Hector G Romero

coast blues

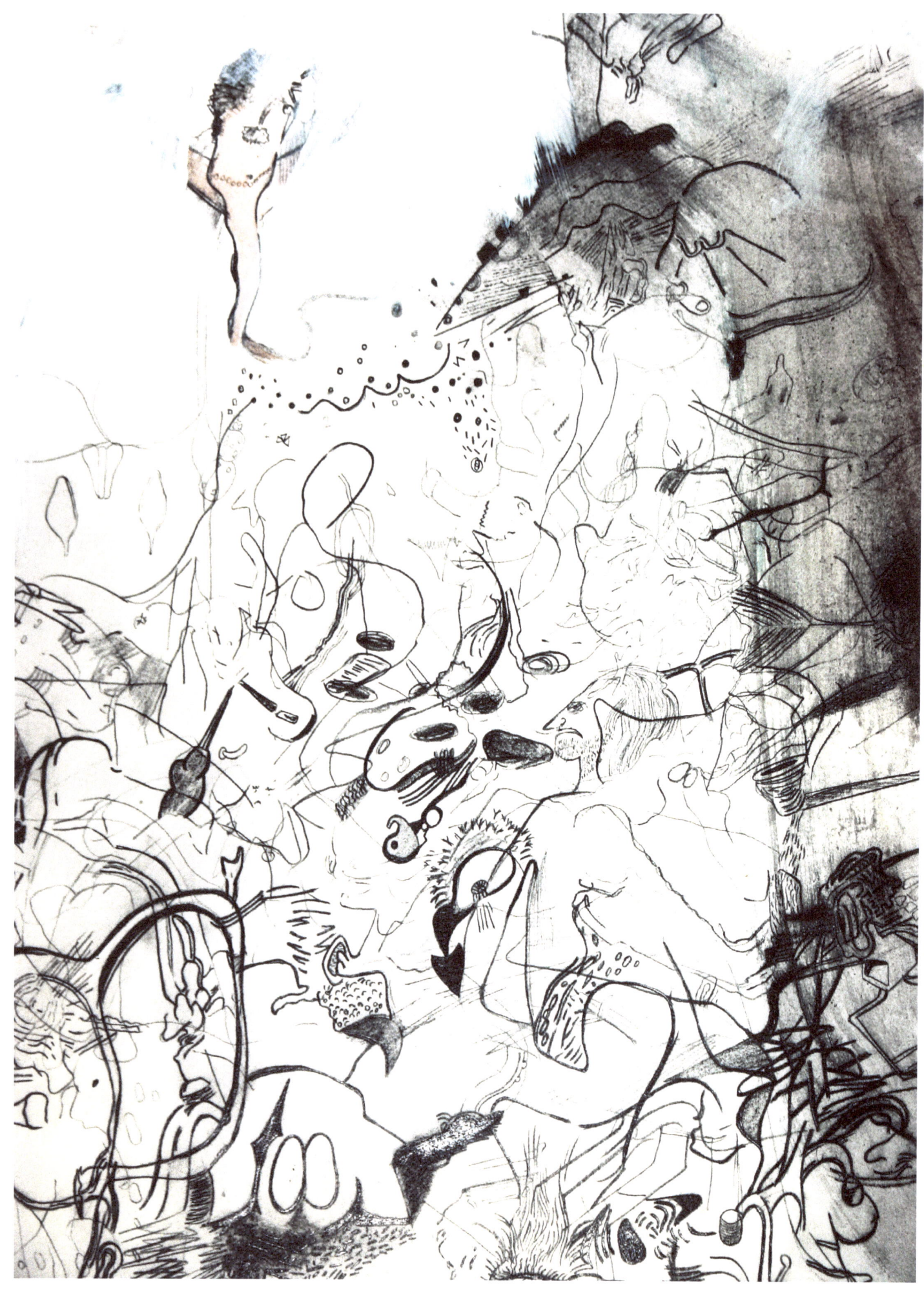

Hector G Romero

coast blues

The Woodside Drawings

NEW DRAWING

VICTORY HALL PRESS

Cult Favorites 30"x 22" mixed media/paper 2010

overleaf detail >

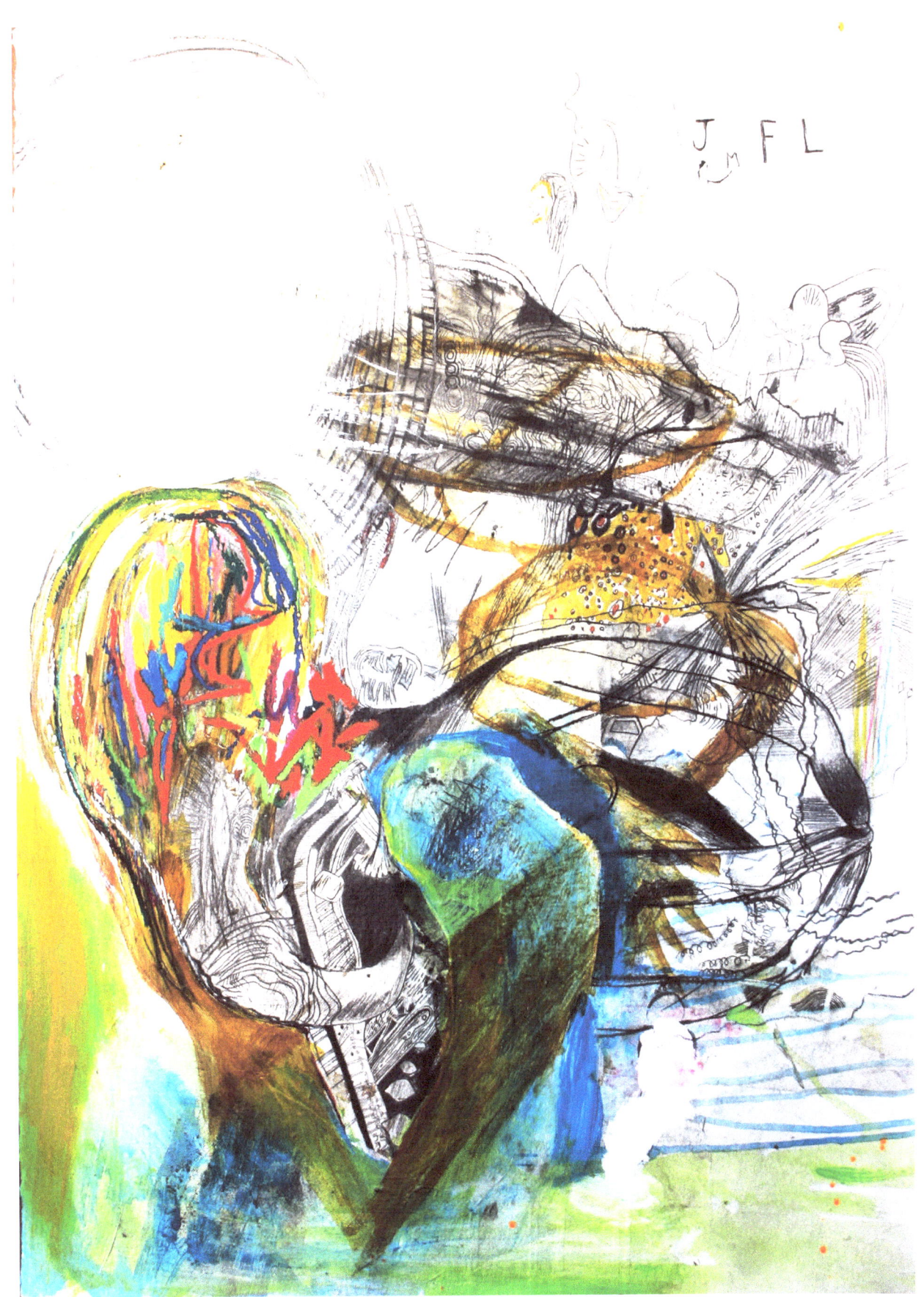

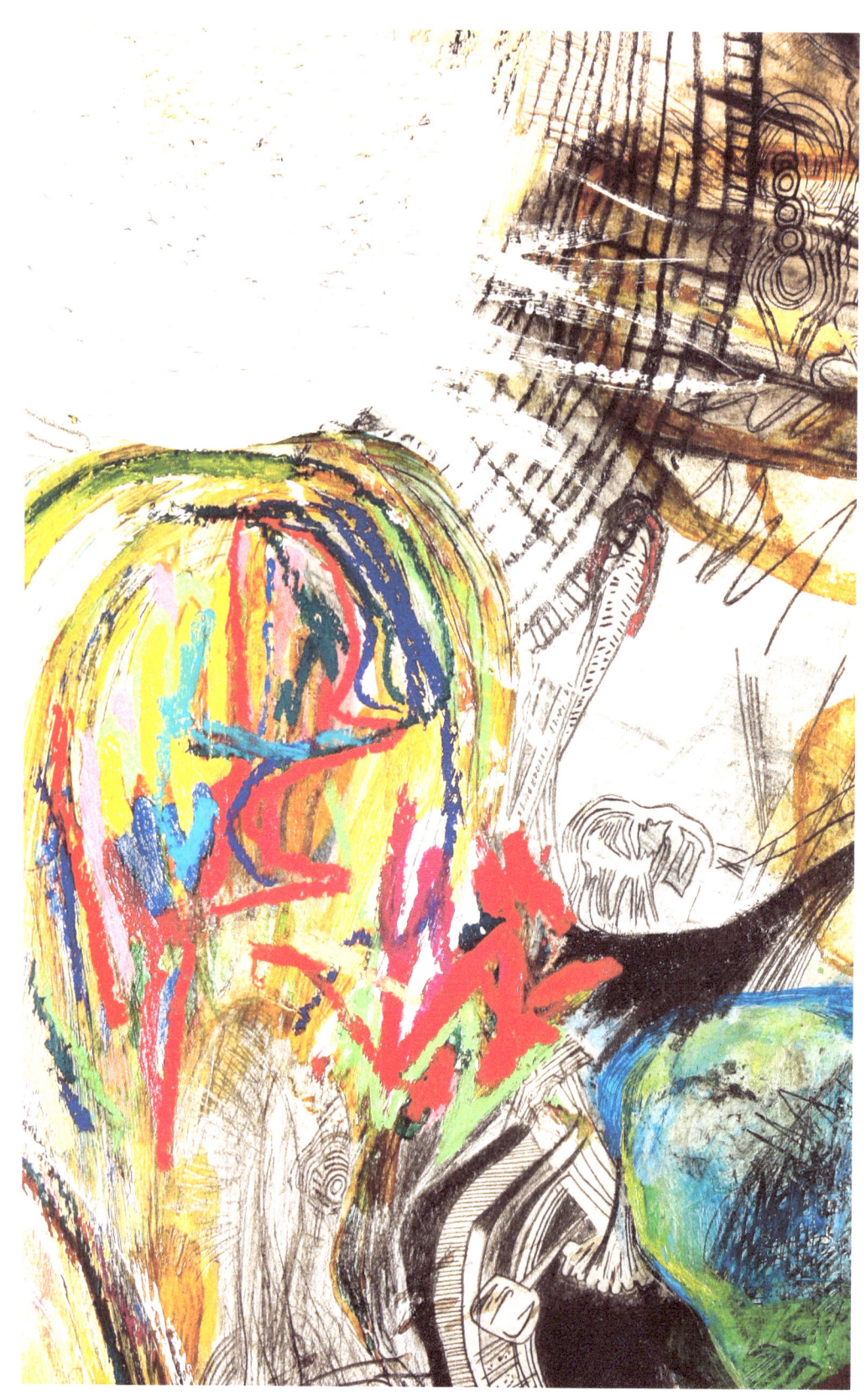

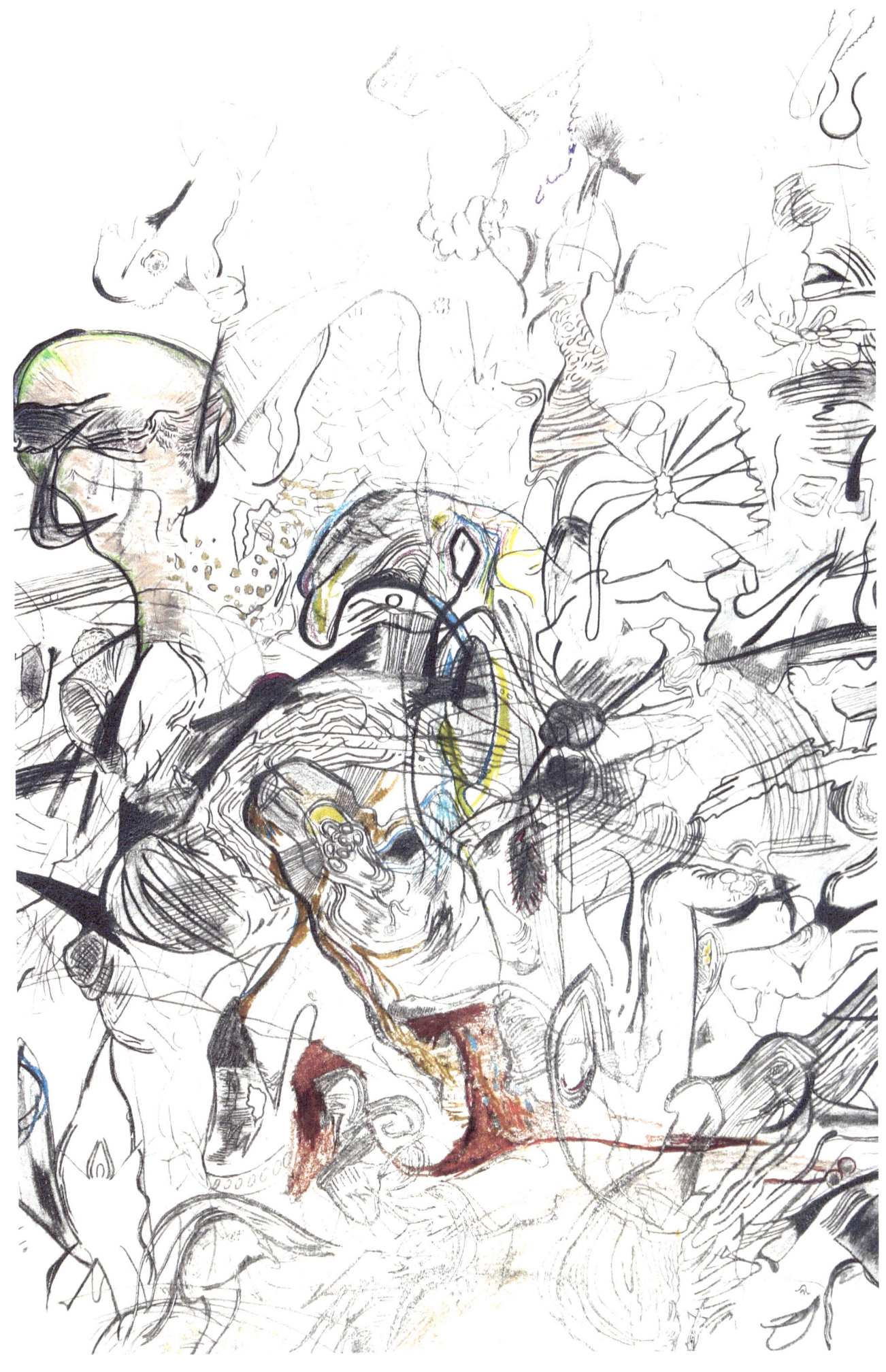

Silly Phase 26"x 20" mixed media/paper 2010

< overleaf detail

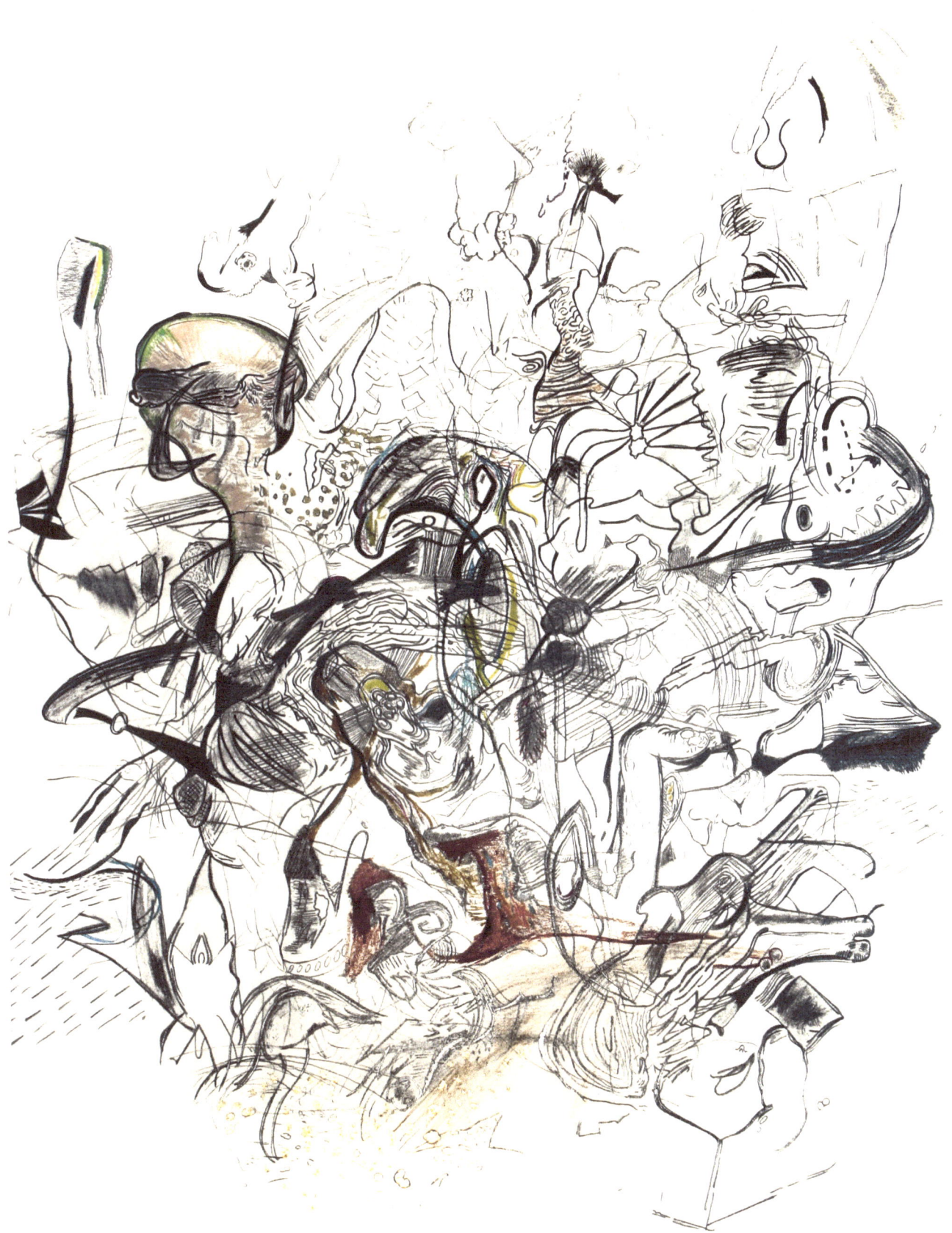

Nemo 30"x 22" mixed media/paper 2010

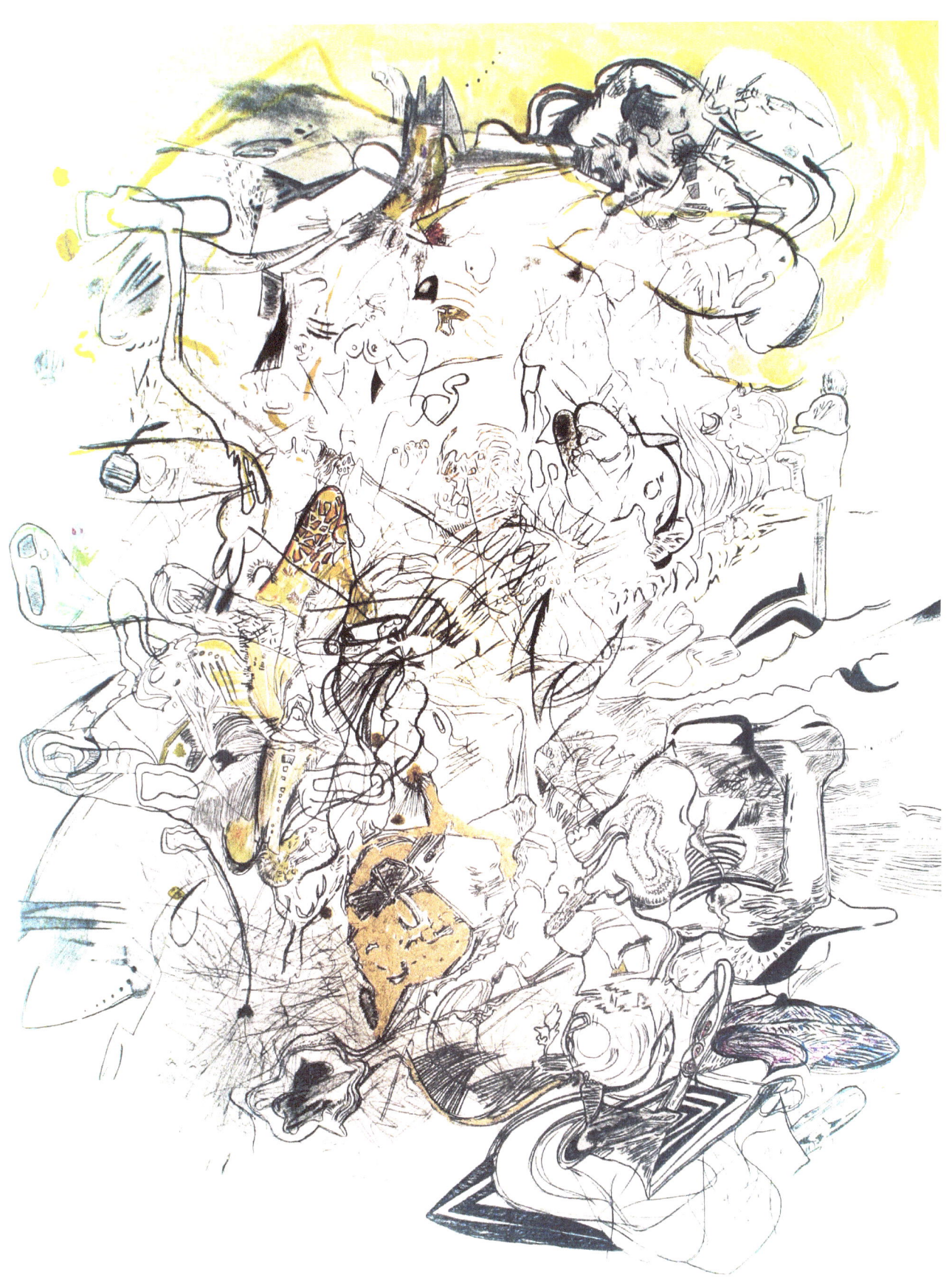

To the Limit 30"x 22" mixed media/paper 2010

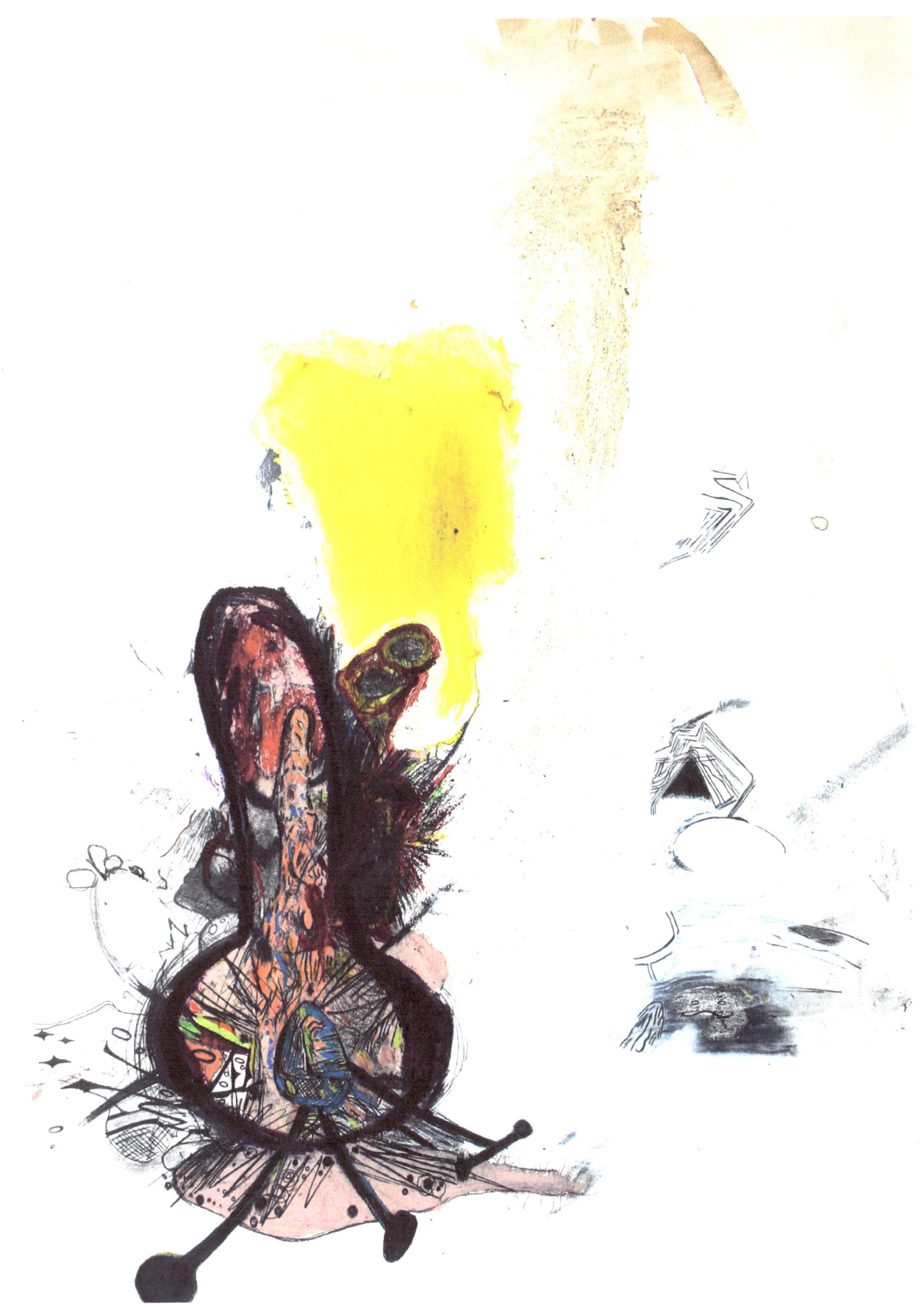

Miracles 30"x 22" mixed media/paper 2010

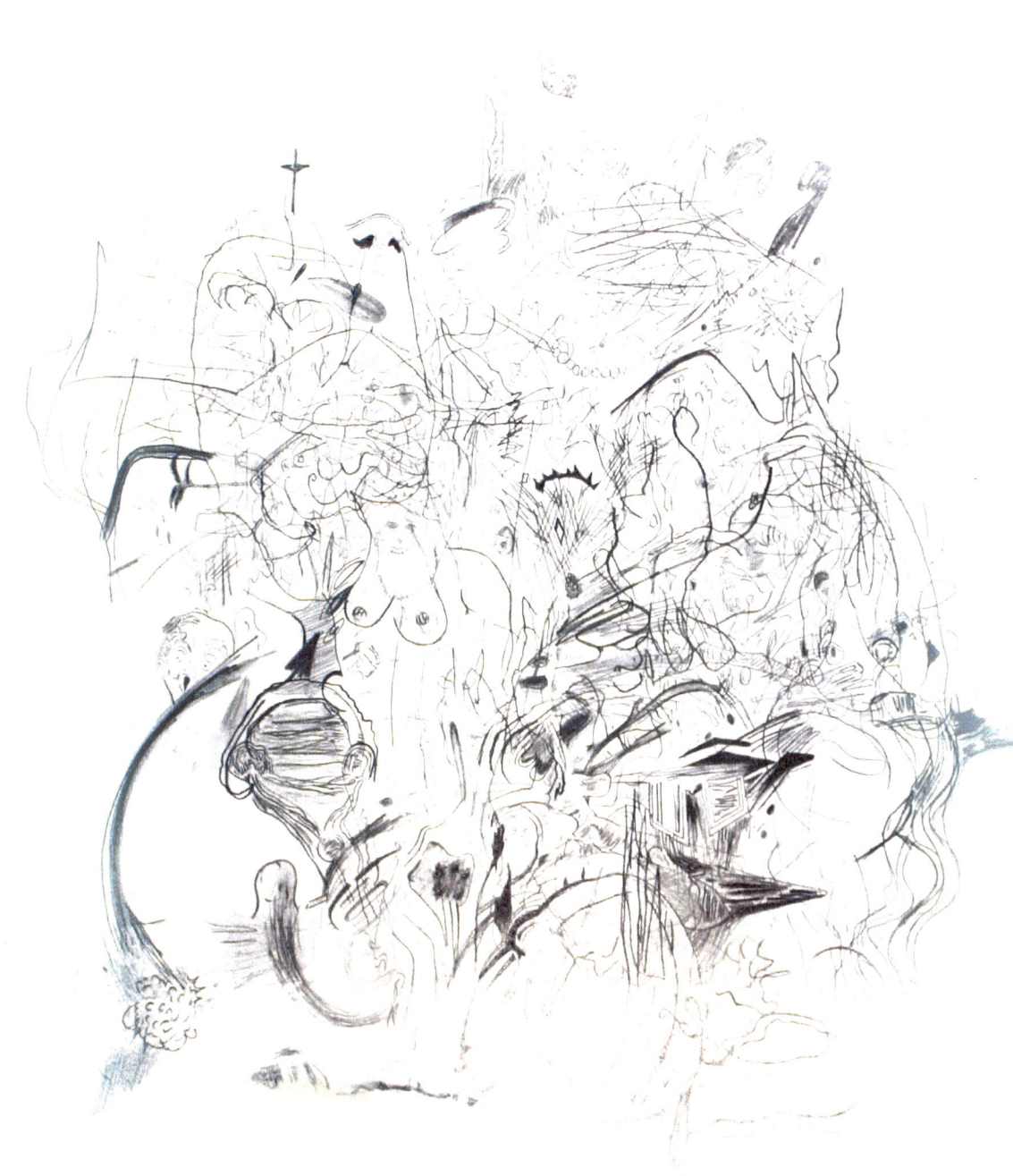

6 valves 30"x 22" mixed media/paper 2010

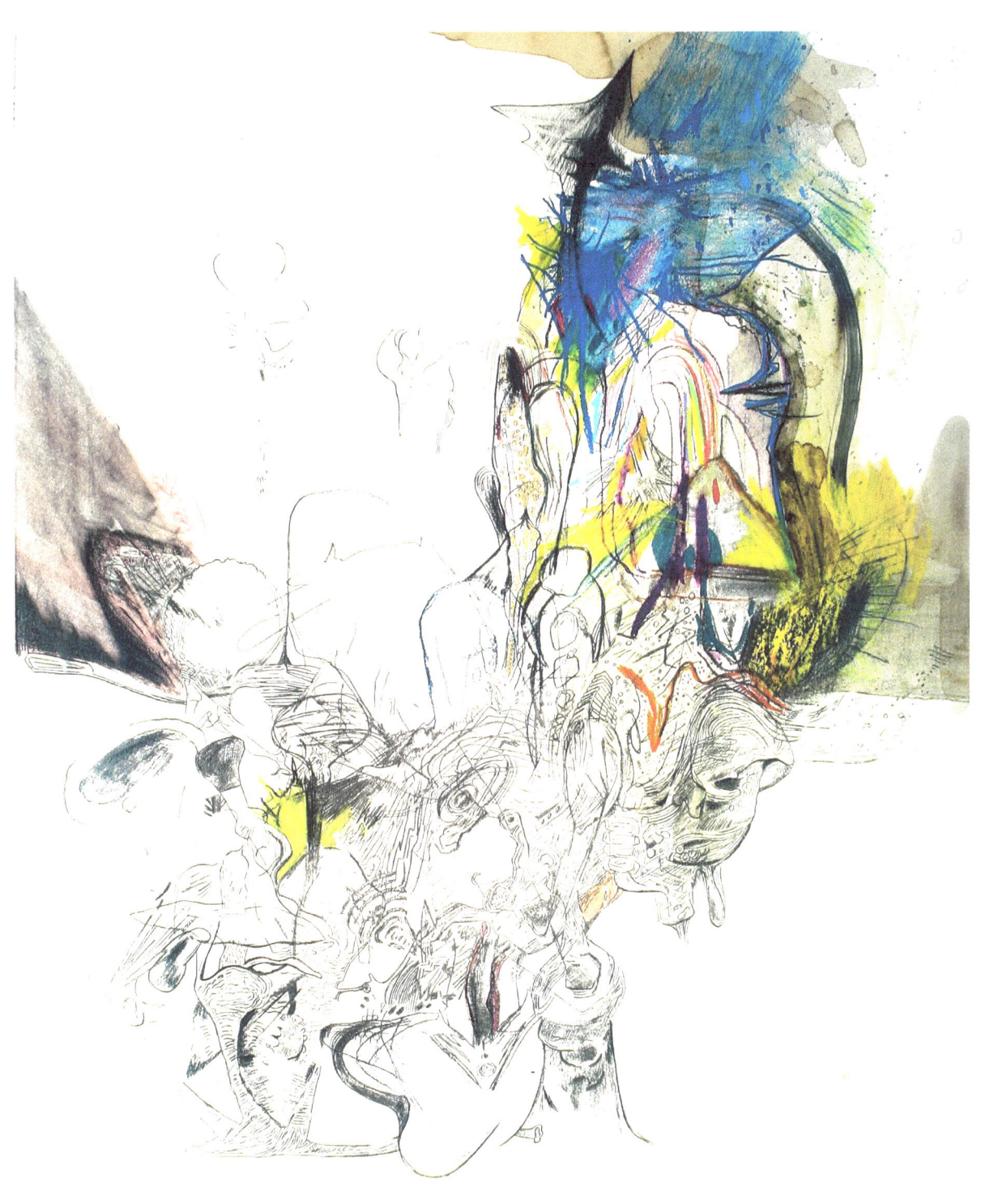

Now Who's Crazy ? 30"x 22" mixed media/paper 2010

overleaf detail >

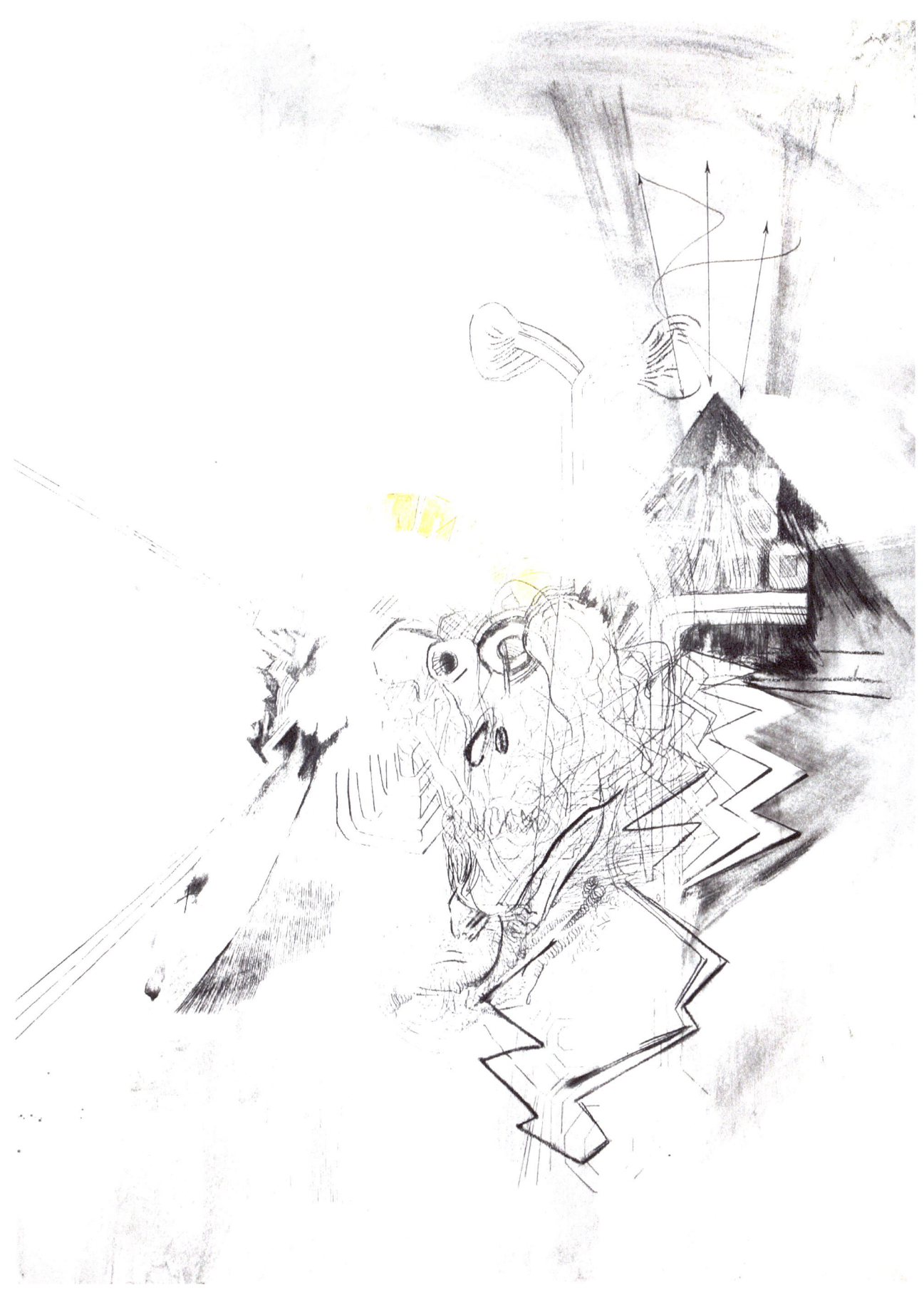

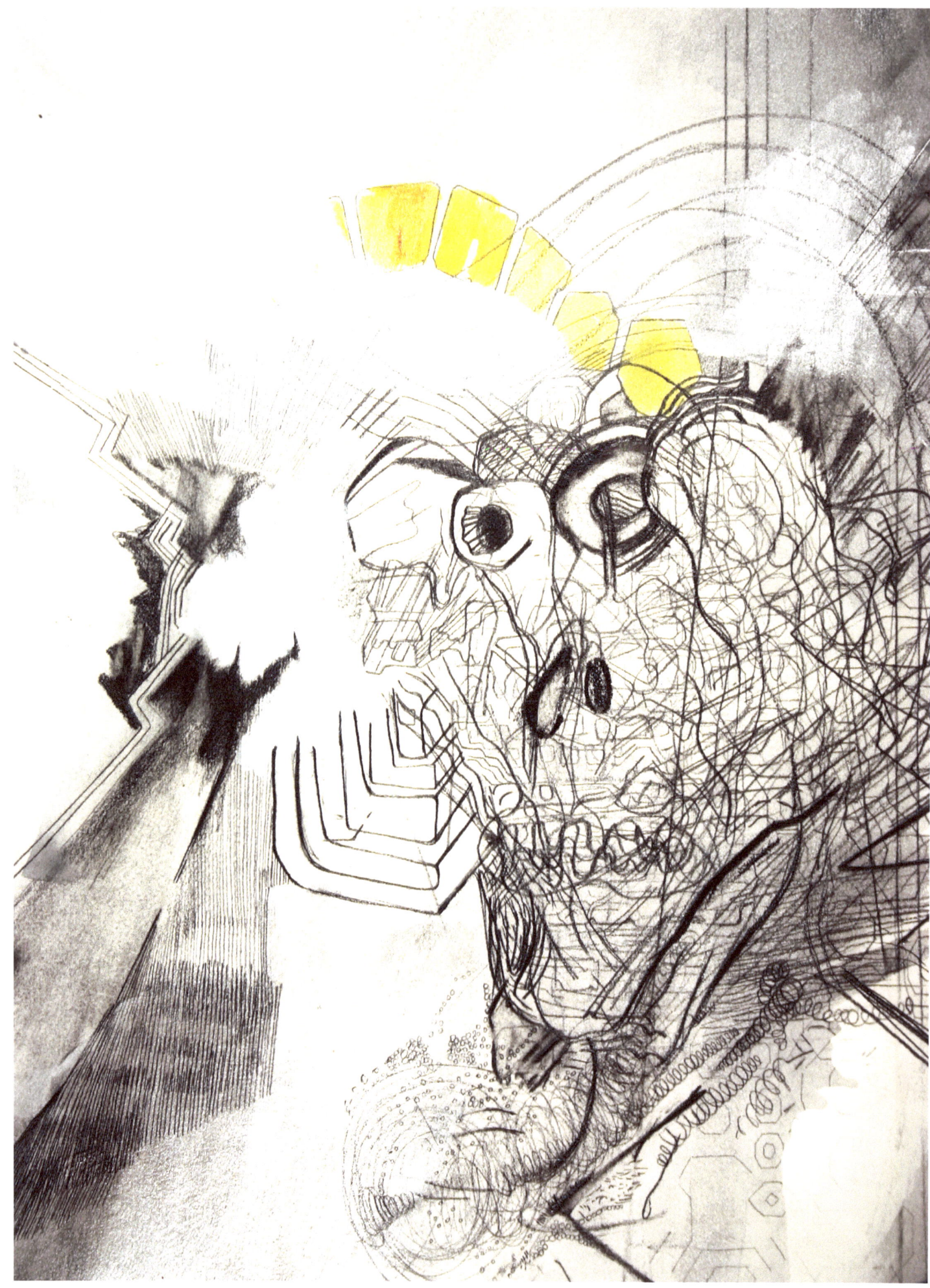

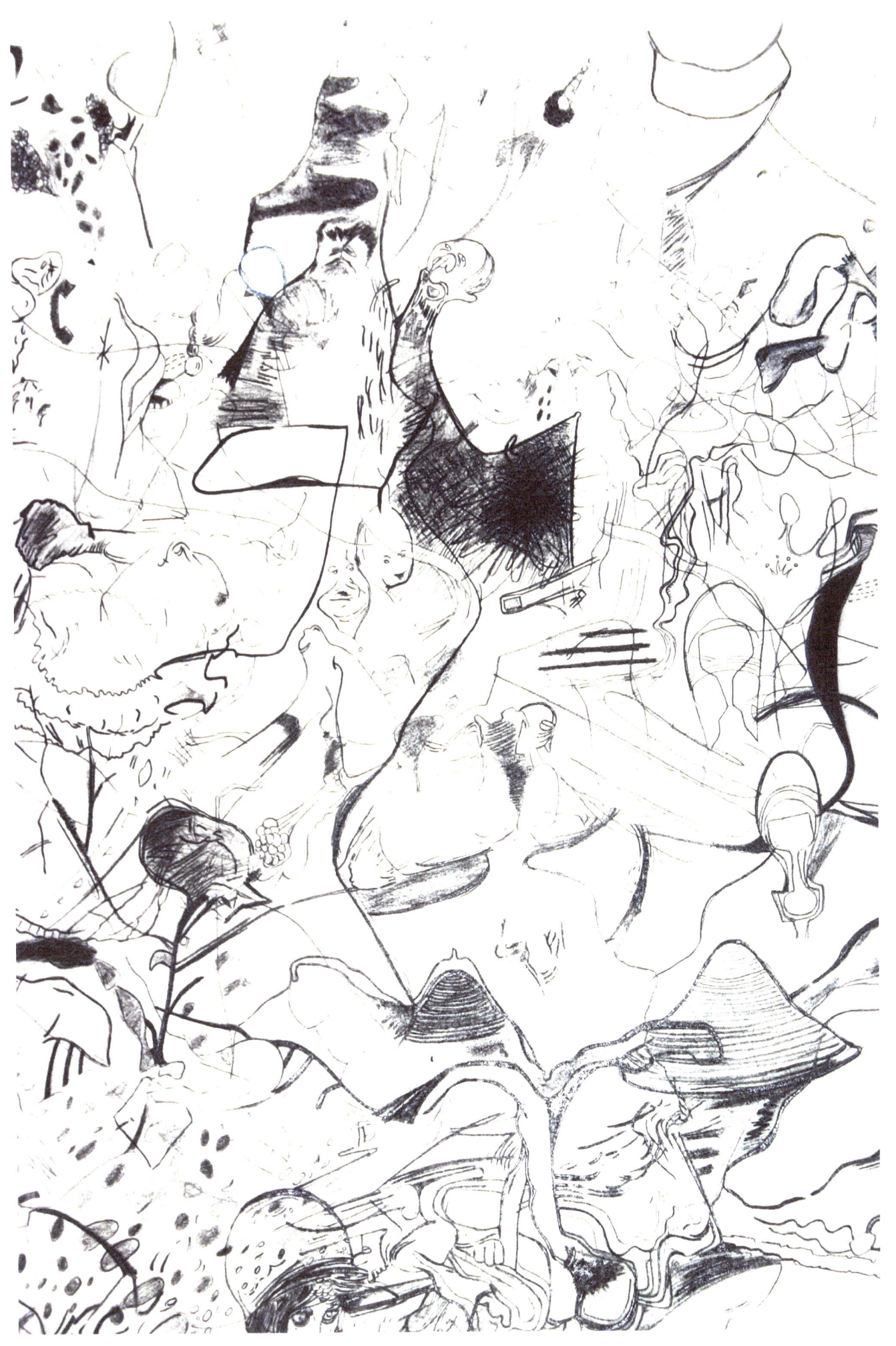

Early Raveen 30"x 22" pencil/paper 2010

< overleaf detail

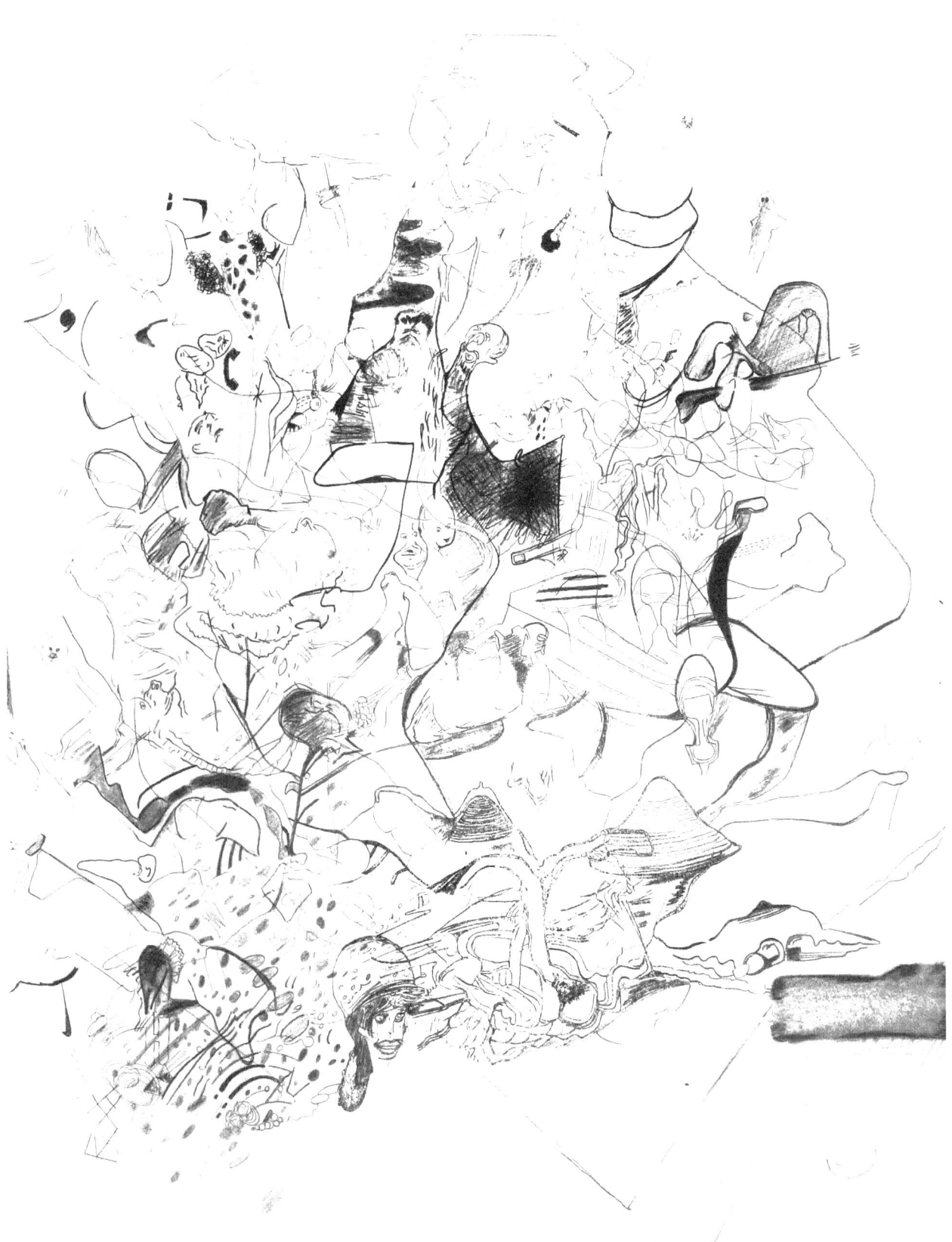

Fat Lip 30"x 22" mixed media/paper 2010

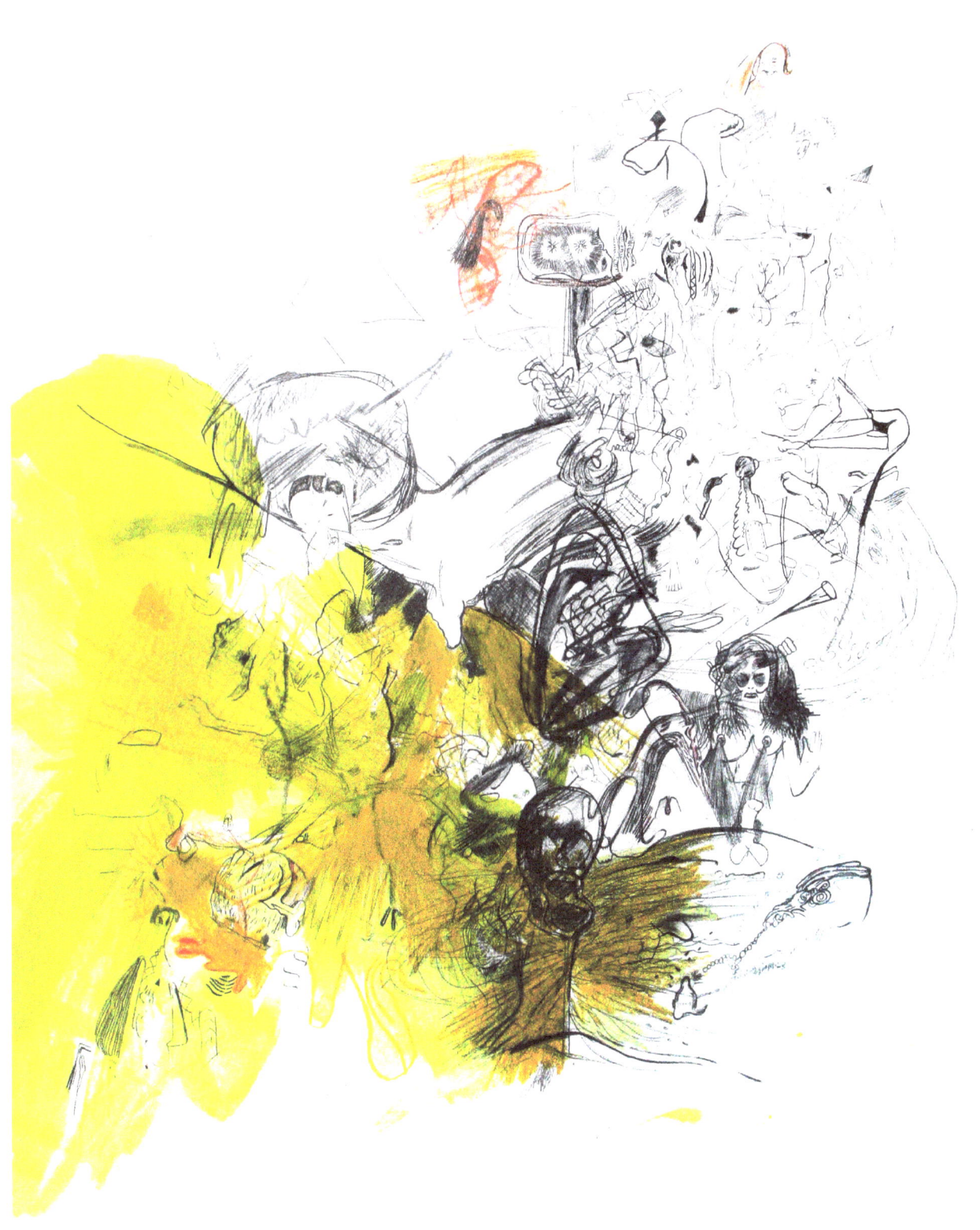

Untitled (Have a Nice Day) 30"x 22" mixed media/paper 2011

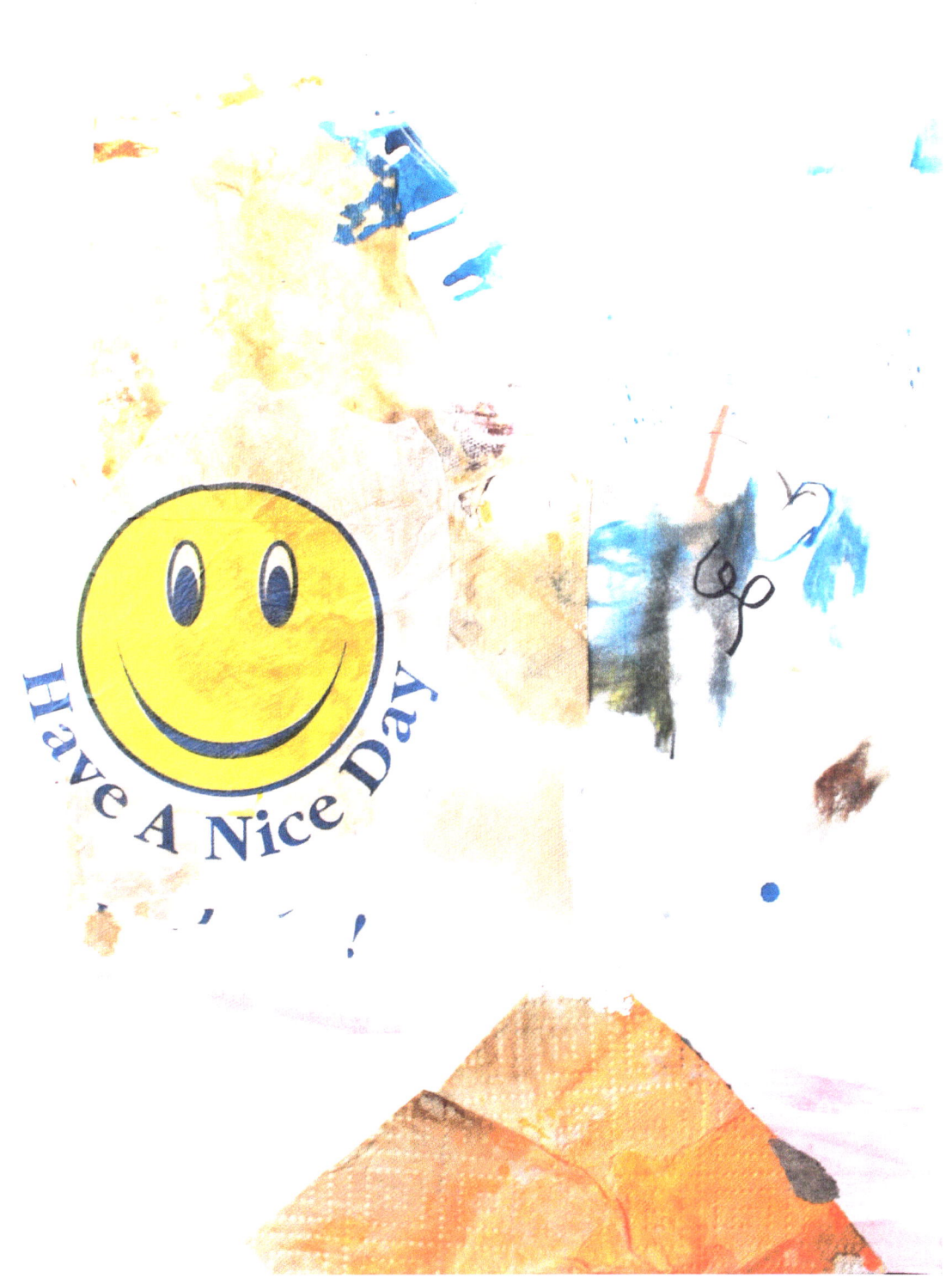

How Do You Feel Today? 28"x 25" acrylic/paper 2011

overleaf detail >

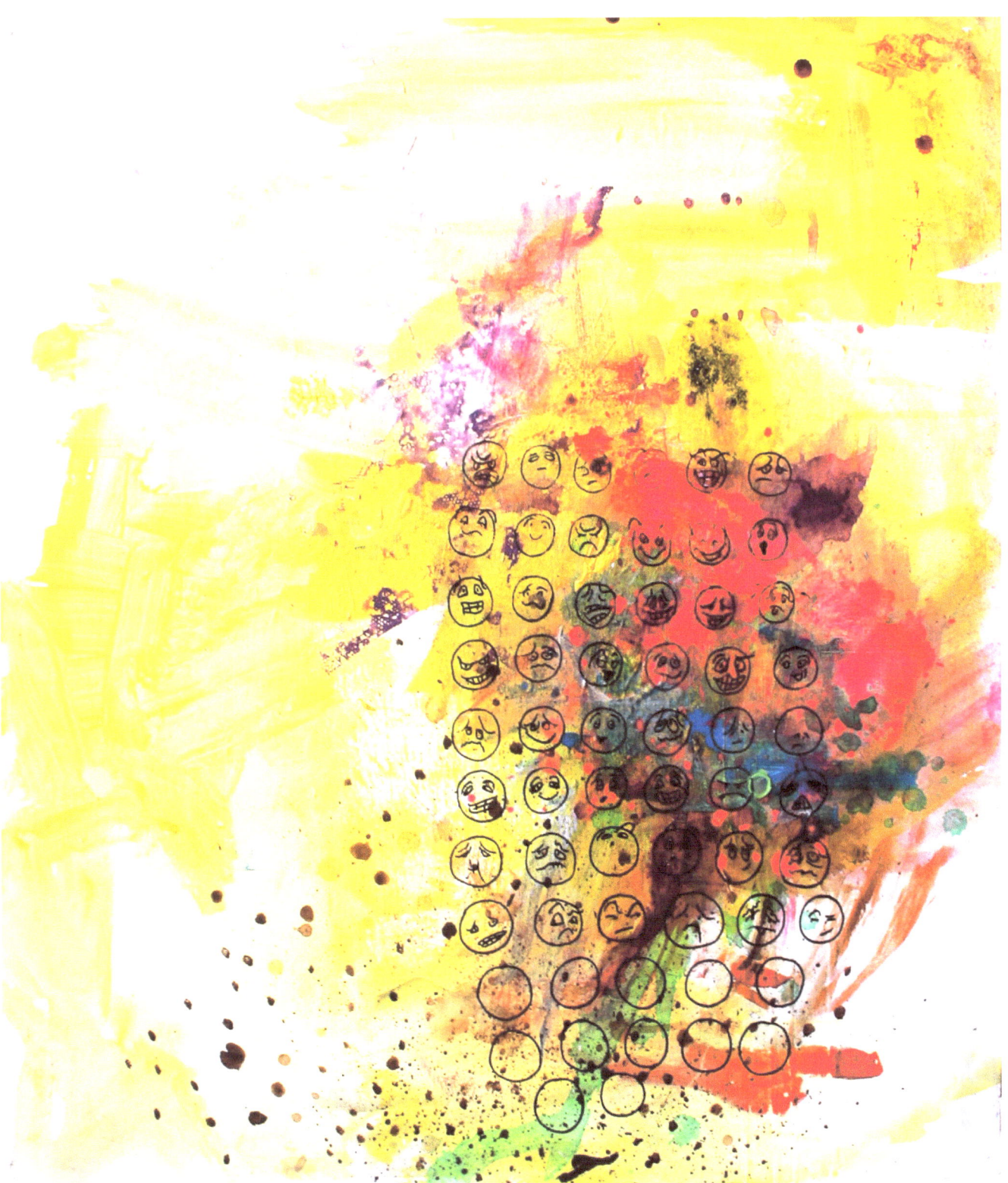

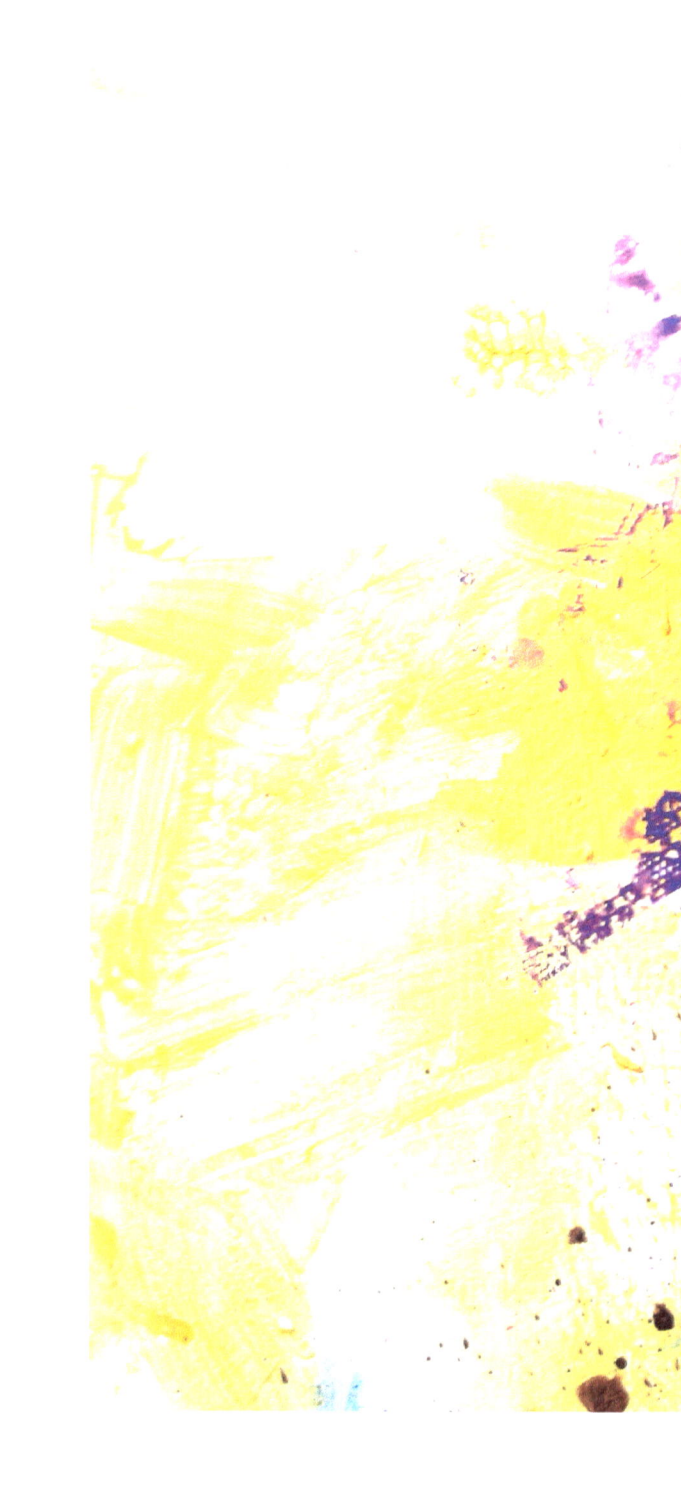

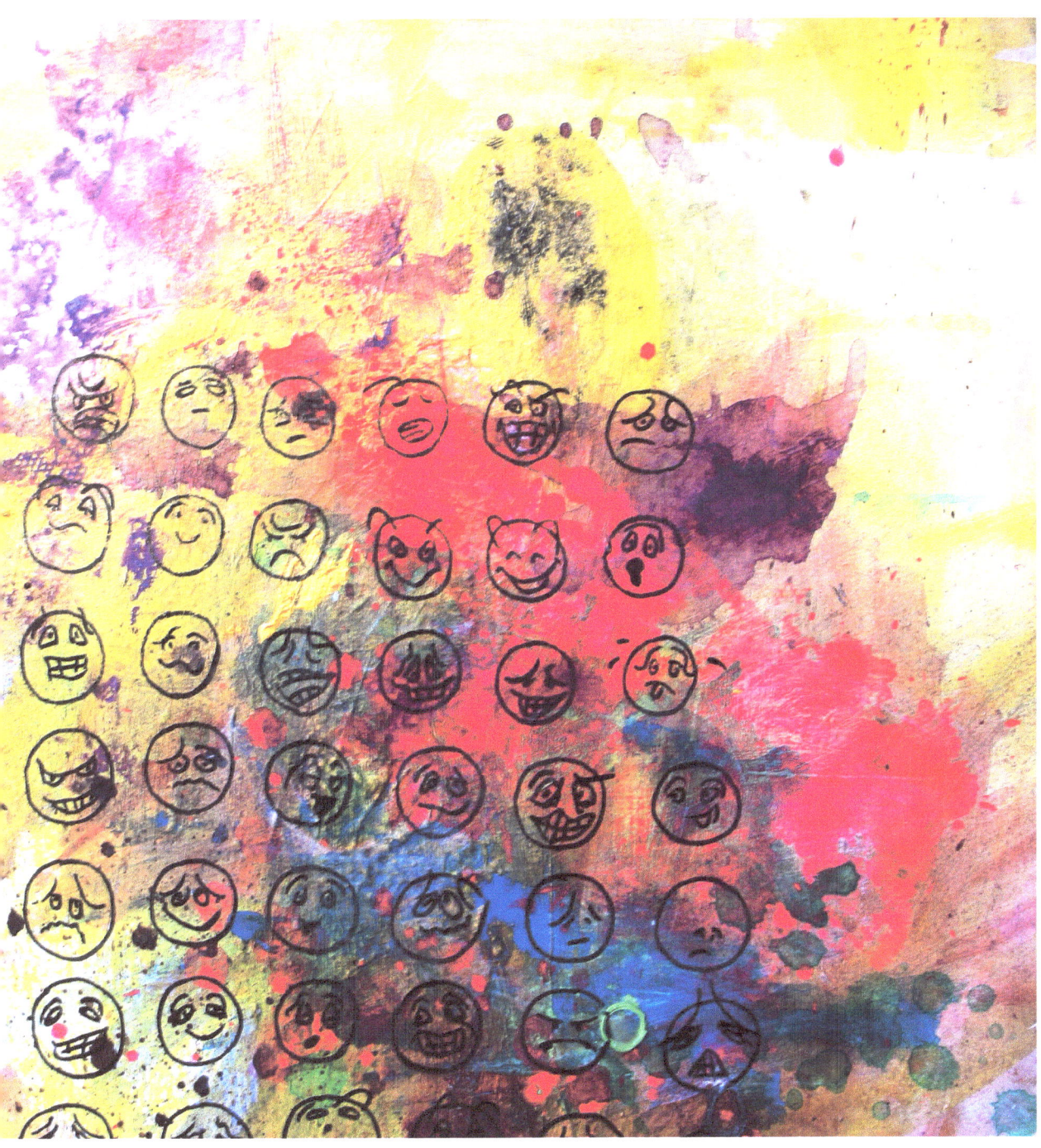

Estereo Vida I 30"x 22" mixed media/paper 2010

overleaf detail, Shangri La 30"x 22" mixed media/paper 2010 >

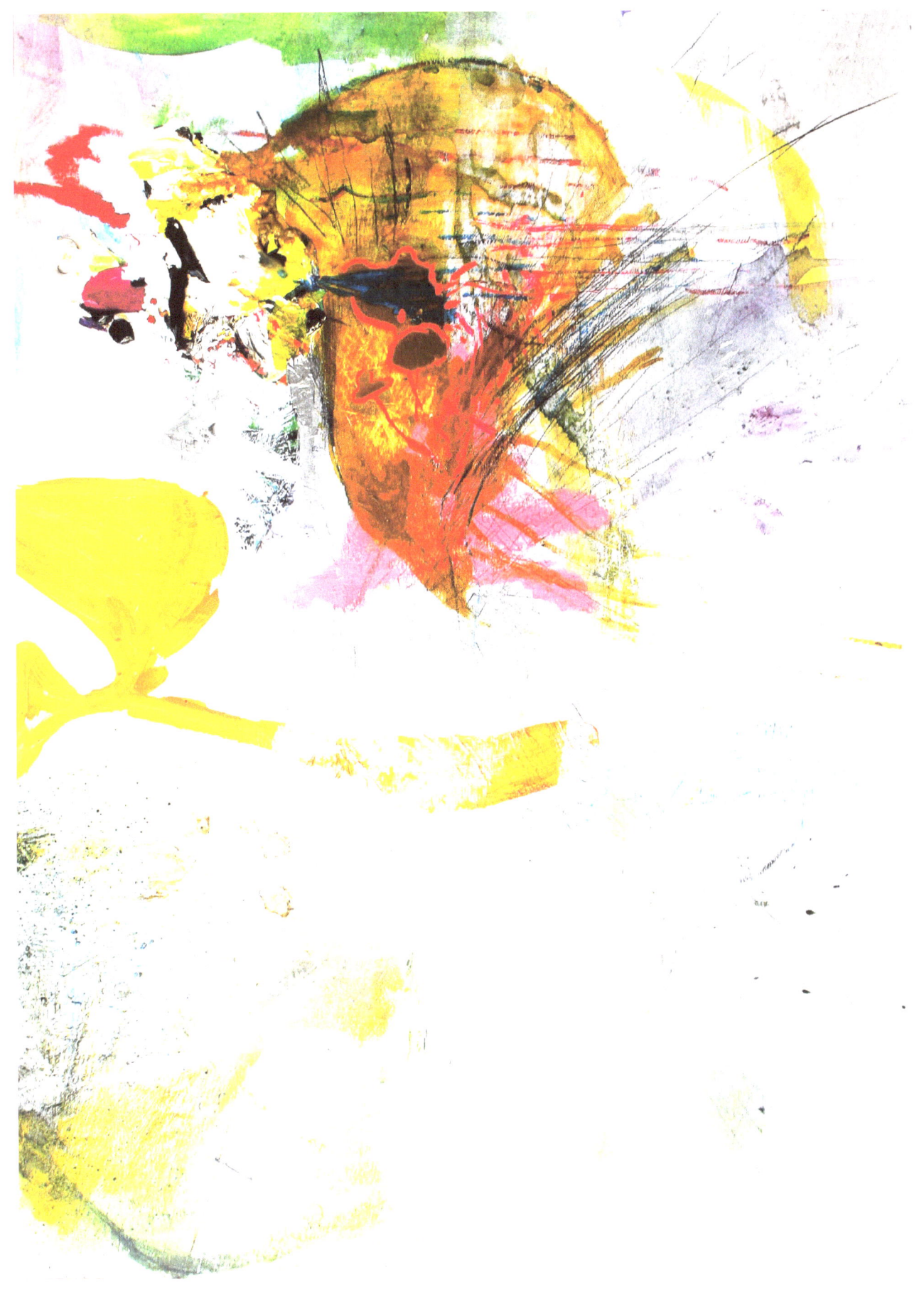

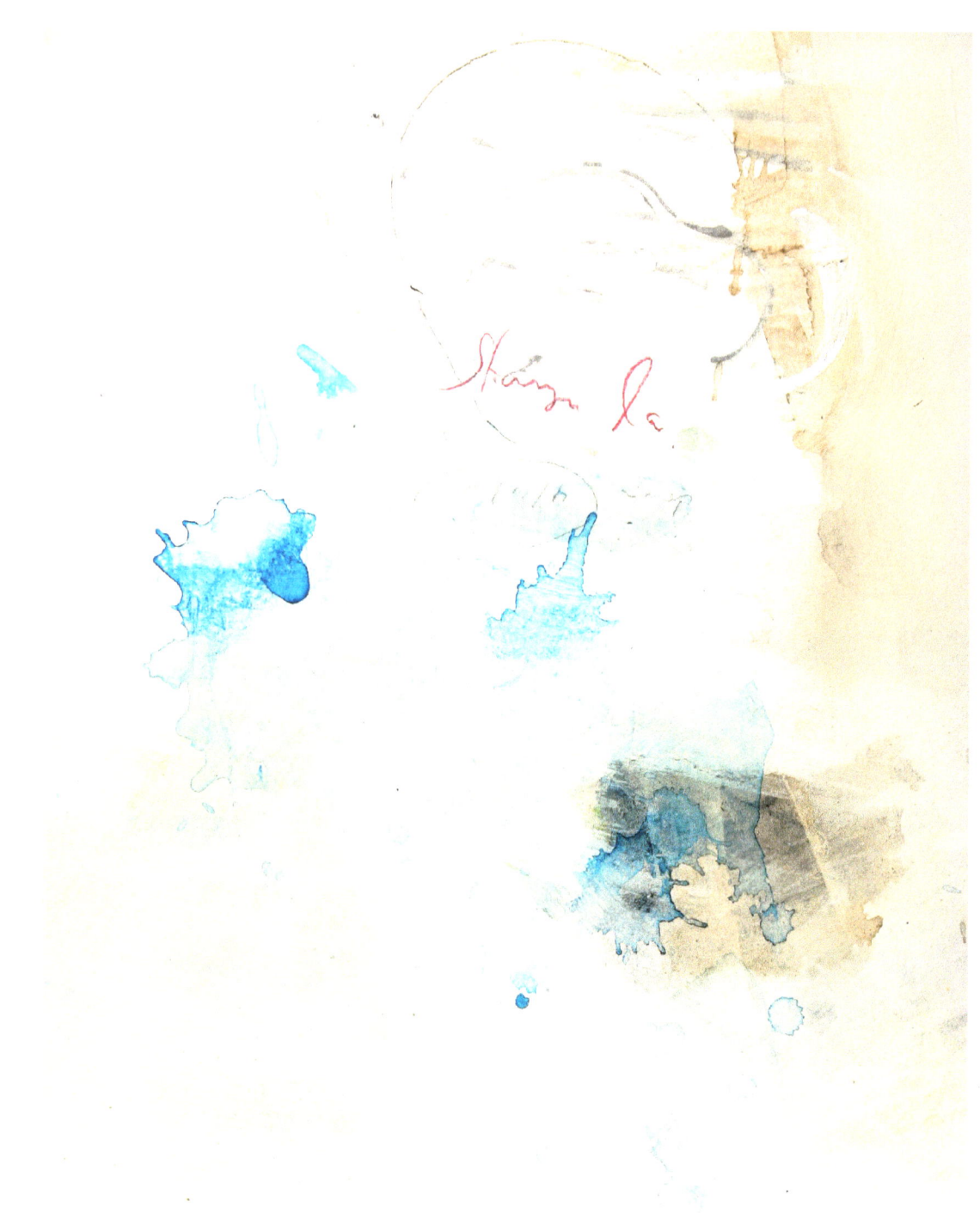

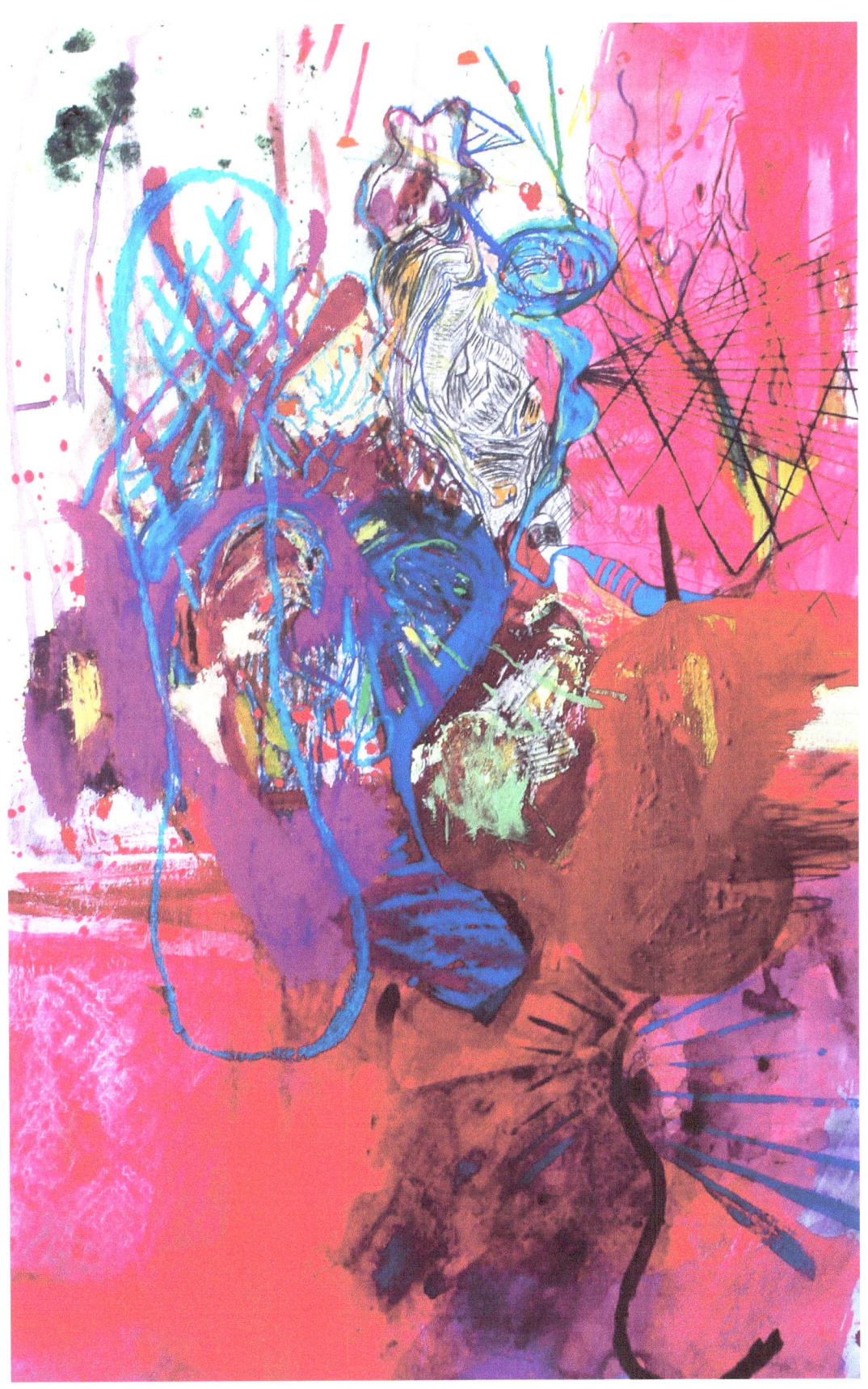

< Estereo Vida II 30"x 22" mixed media/paper 2011 overleaf detail

k.d.i. 30"x 22" pencil/paper 2011

overleaf details >

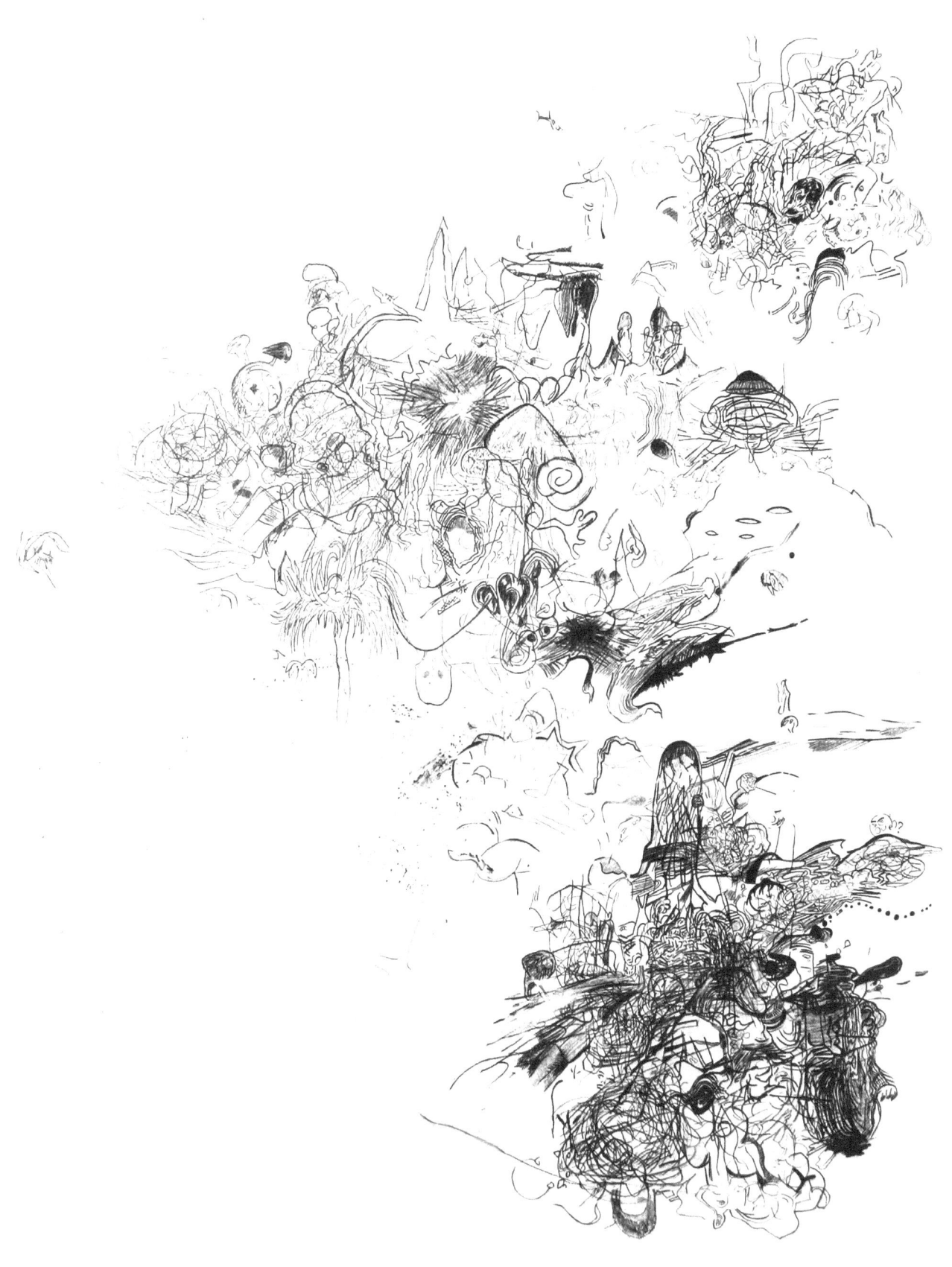

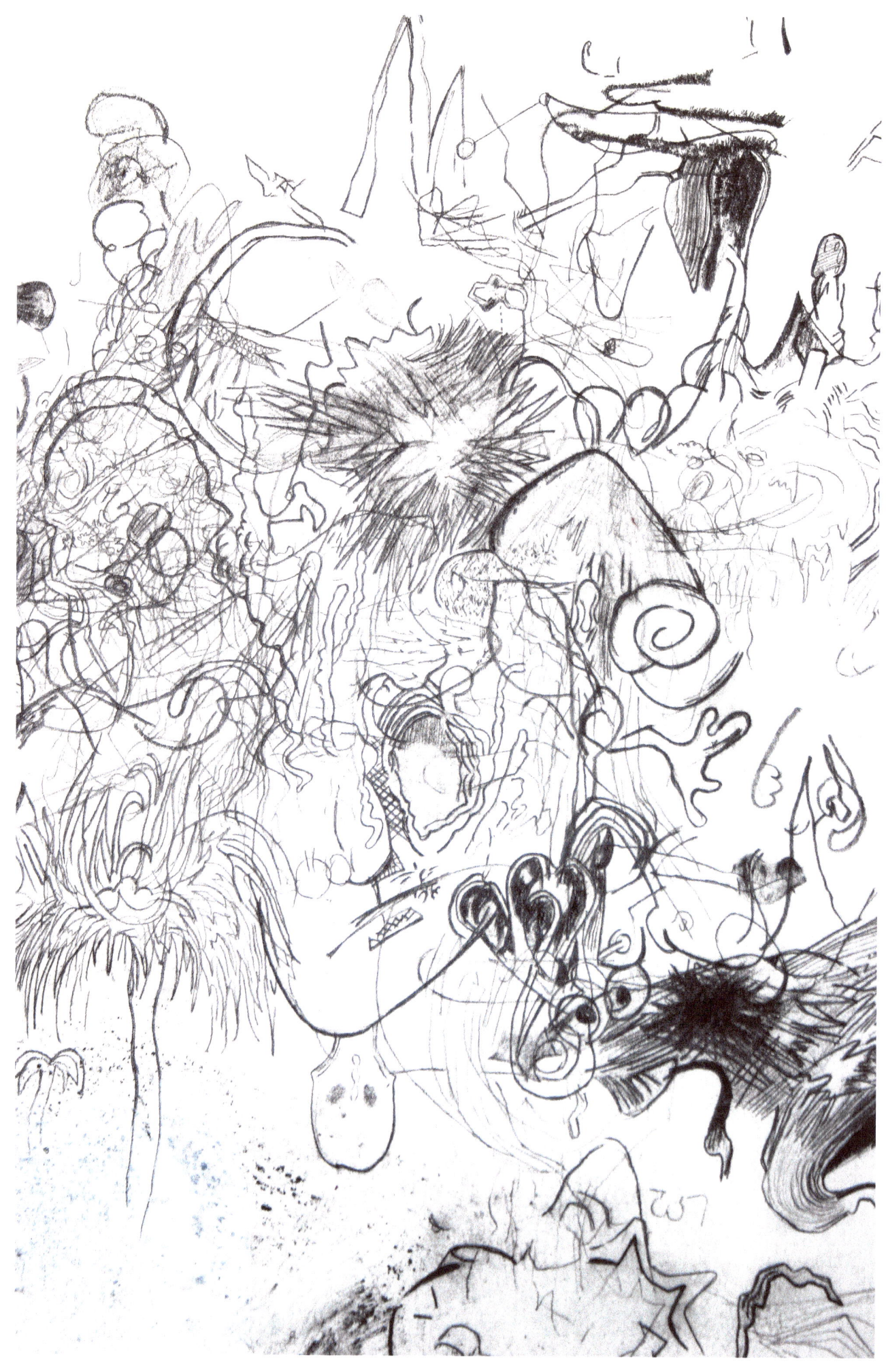

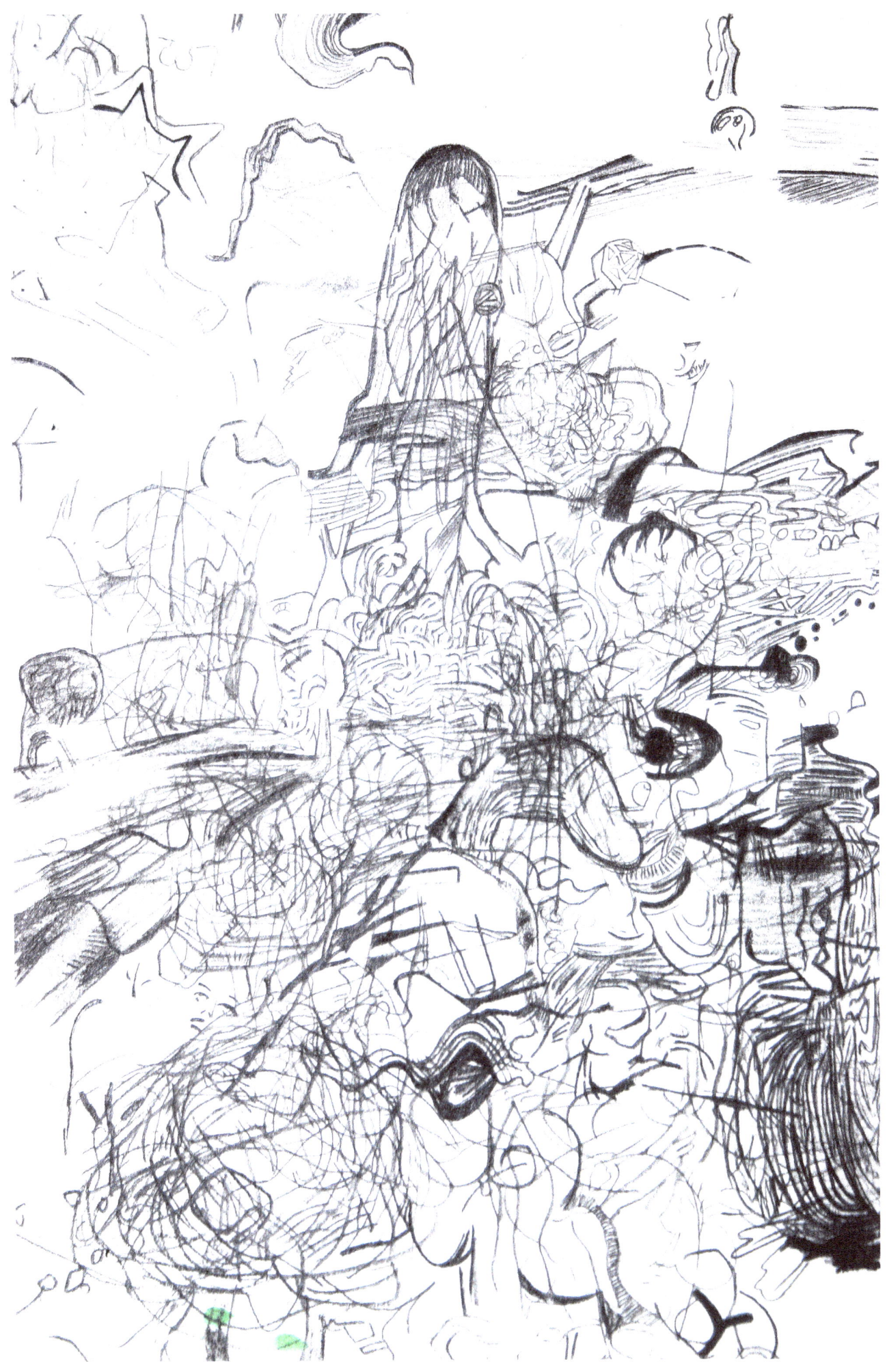

There Will Come a Time I 30" x22" pencil/paper 2011

overleaf detail >

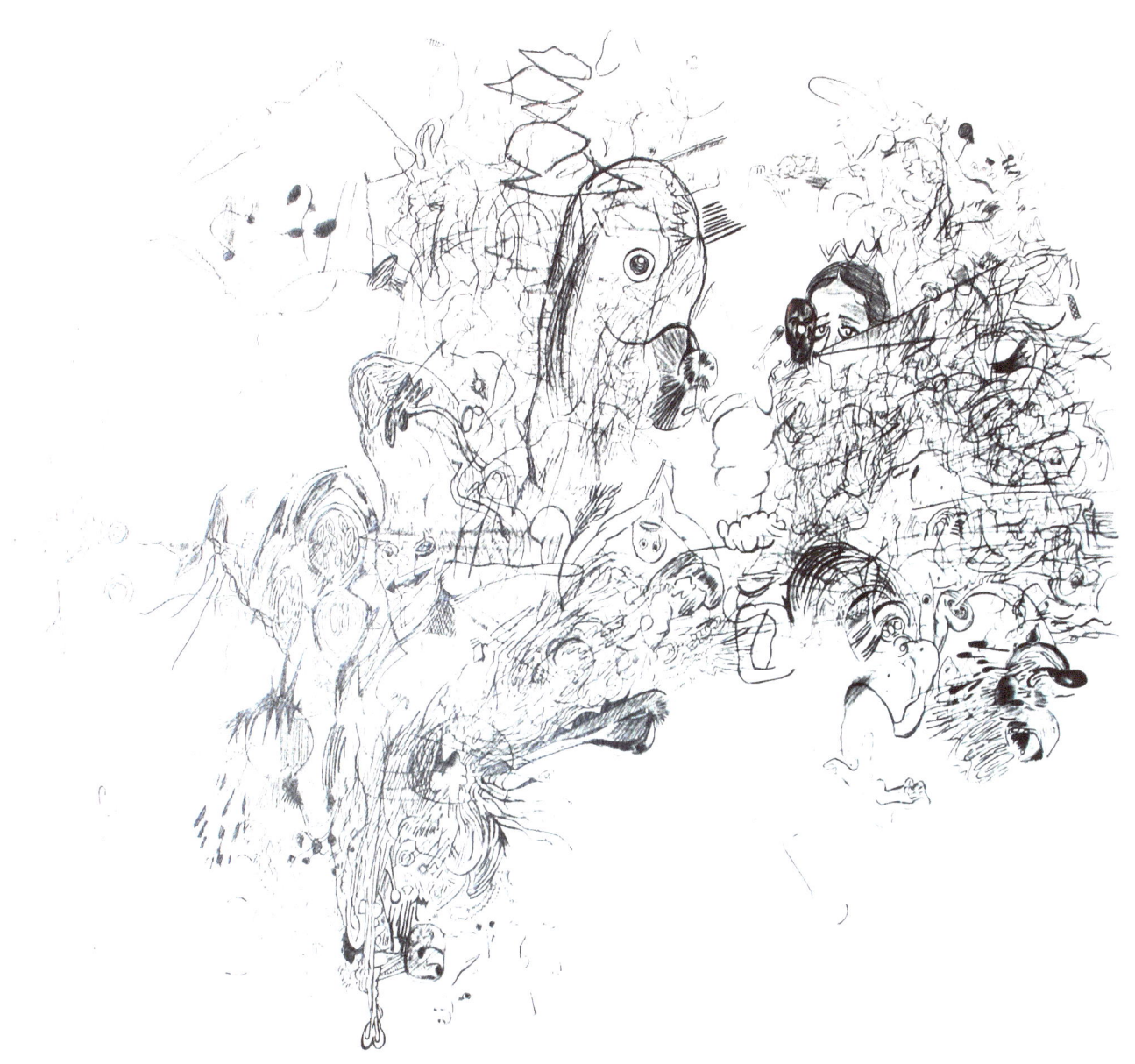

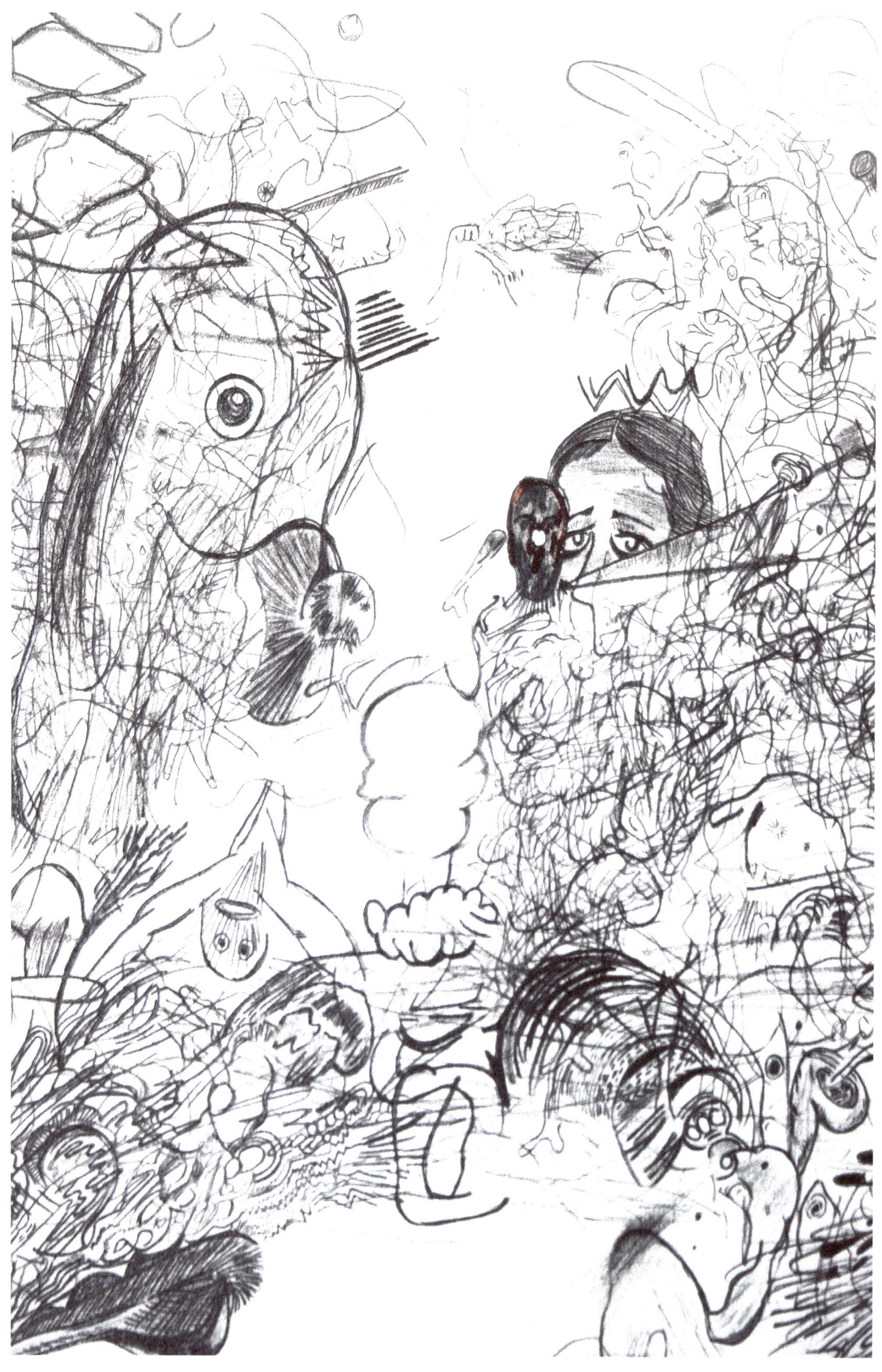

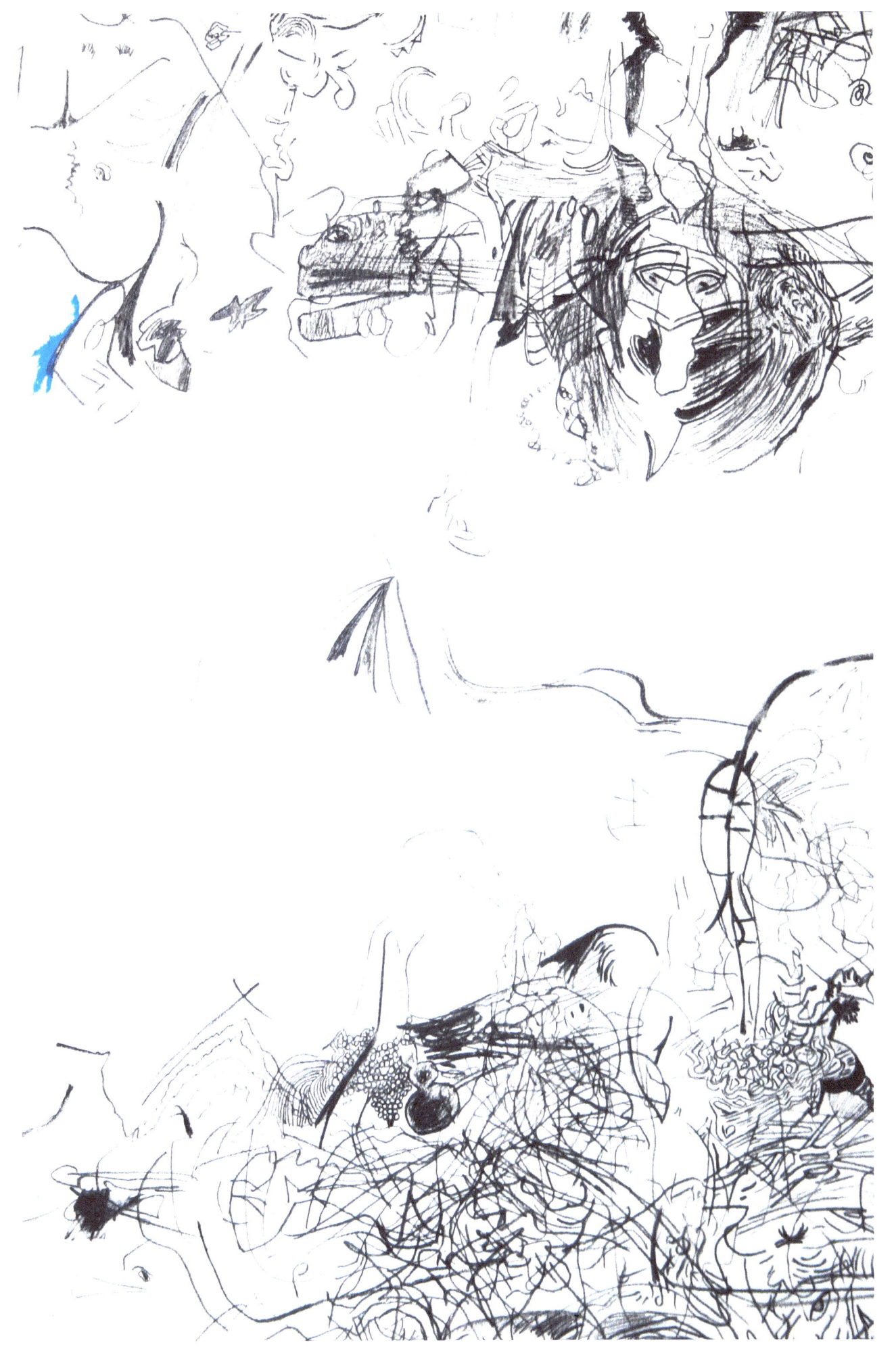

Follow Me 30"x 22" mixed media/paper 2011

< overleaf detail

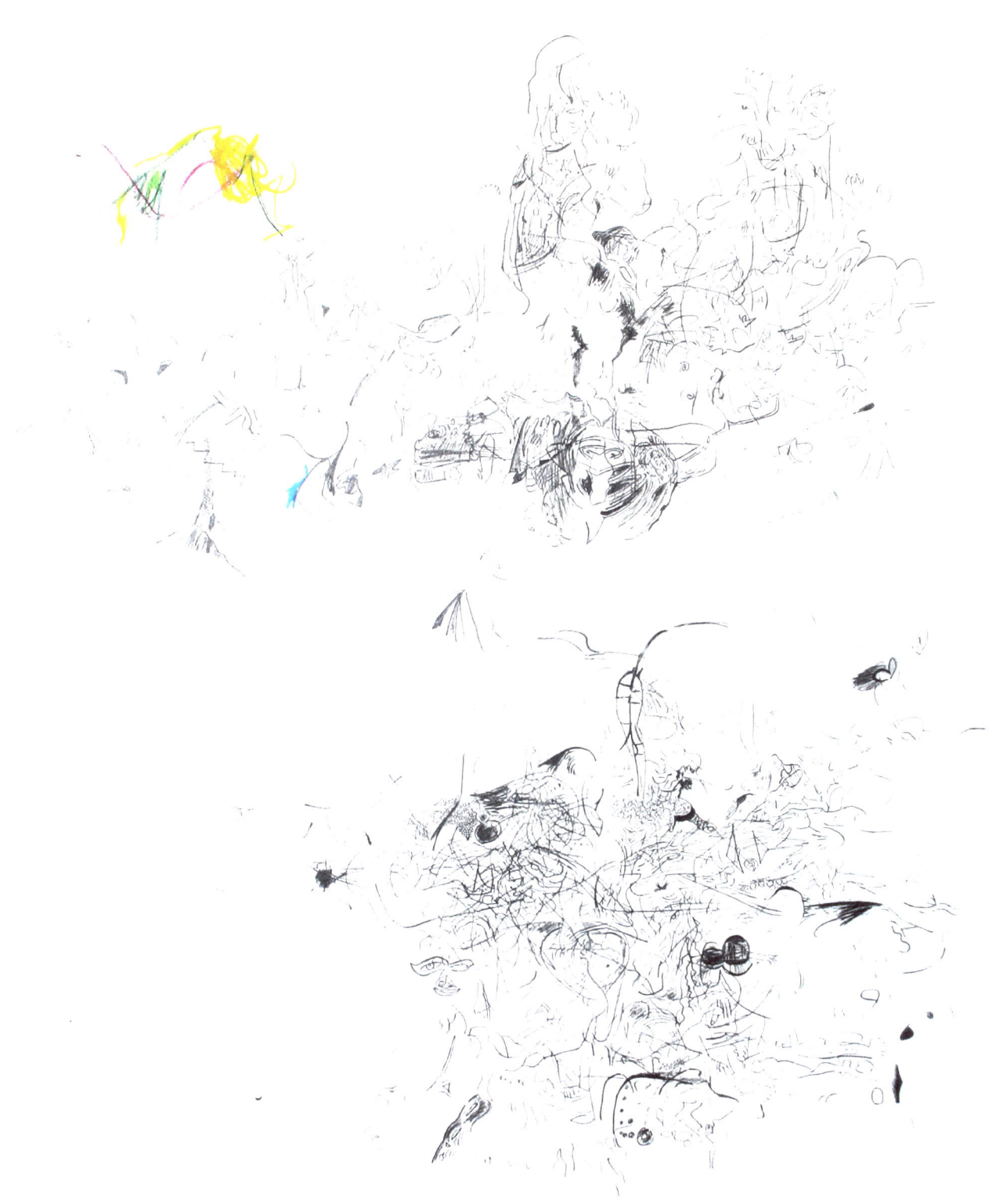

The Weird and the Easy 30"x 22" pencil/paper 2011

overleaf detail >

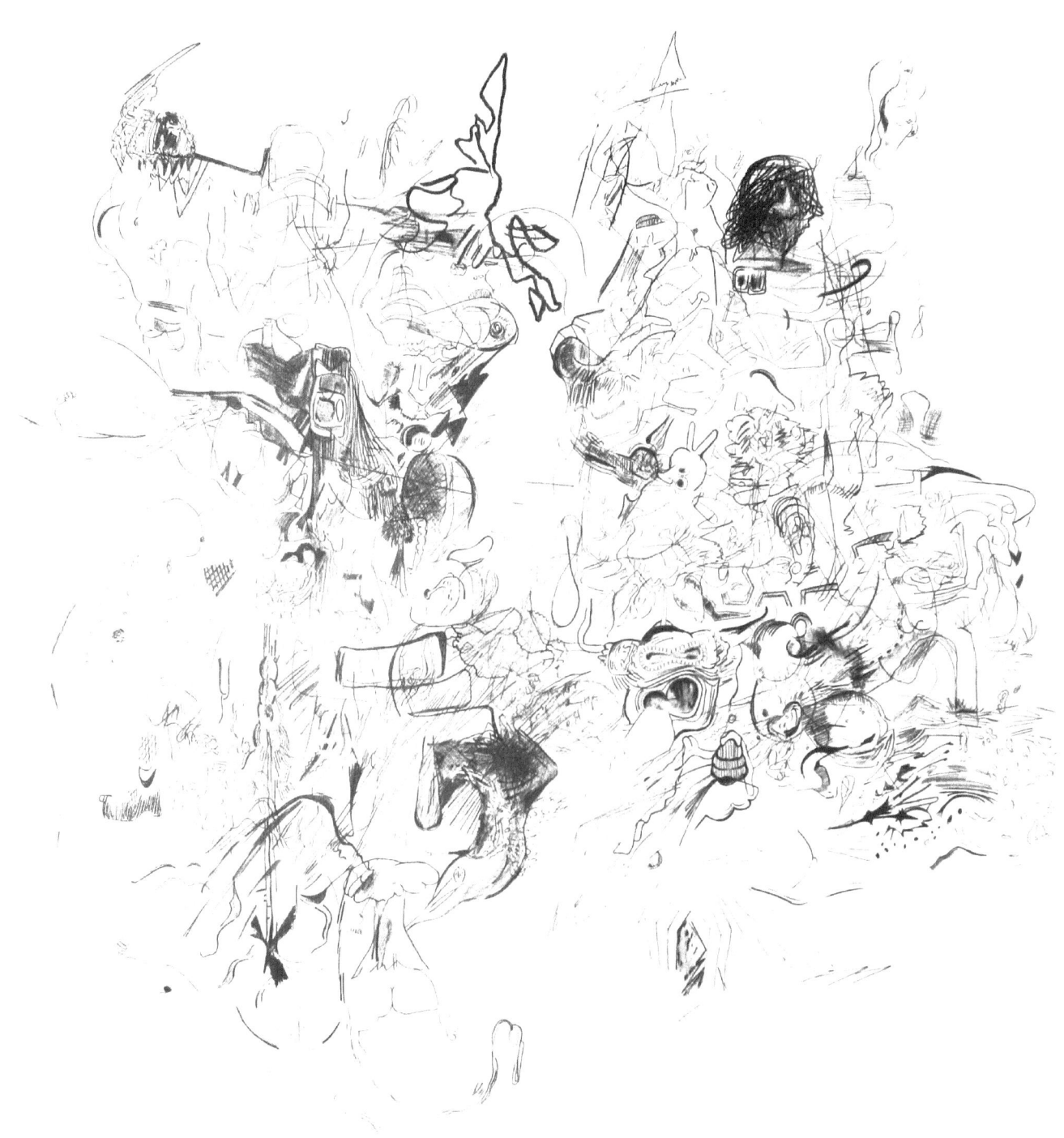

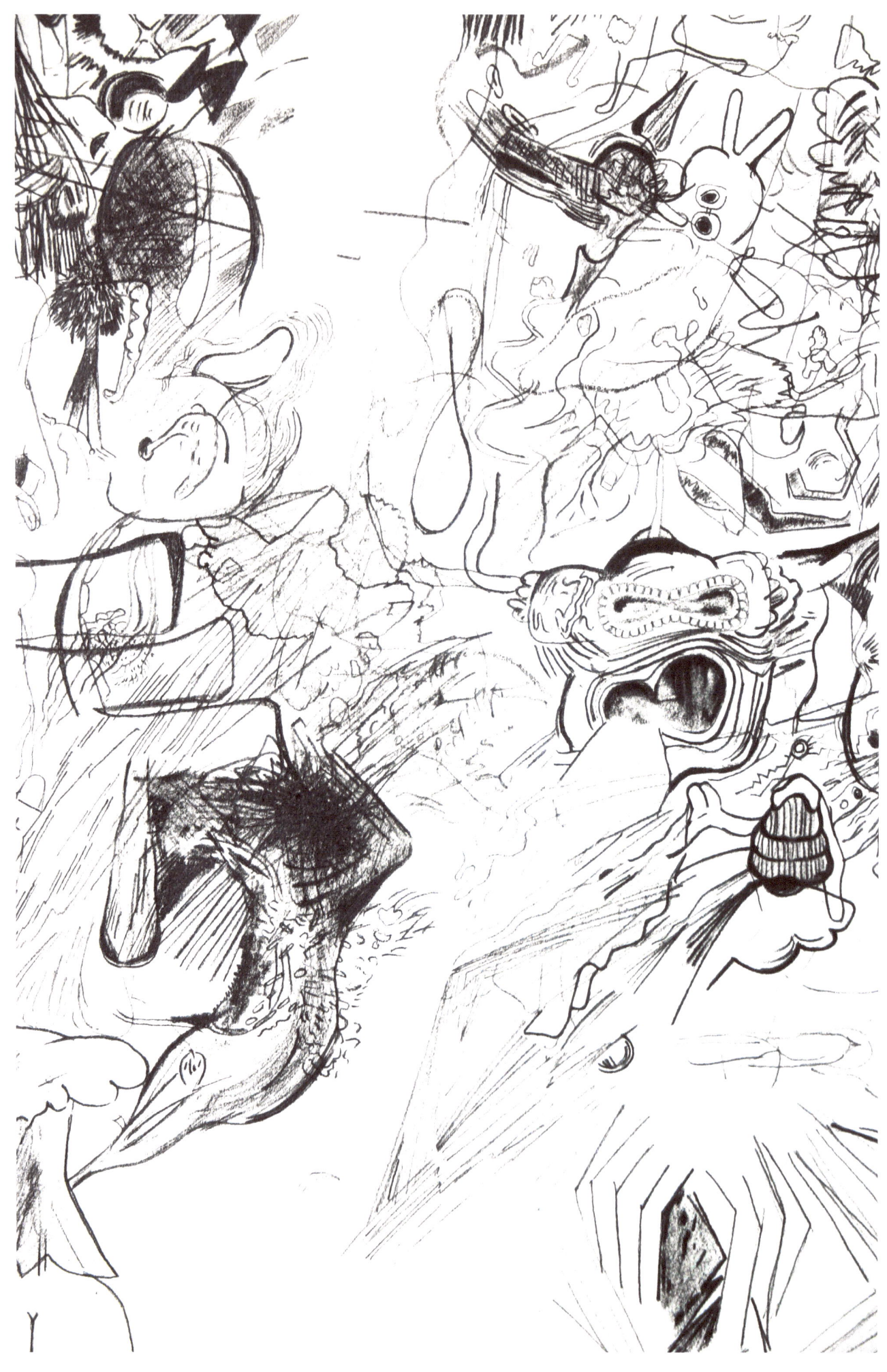

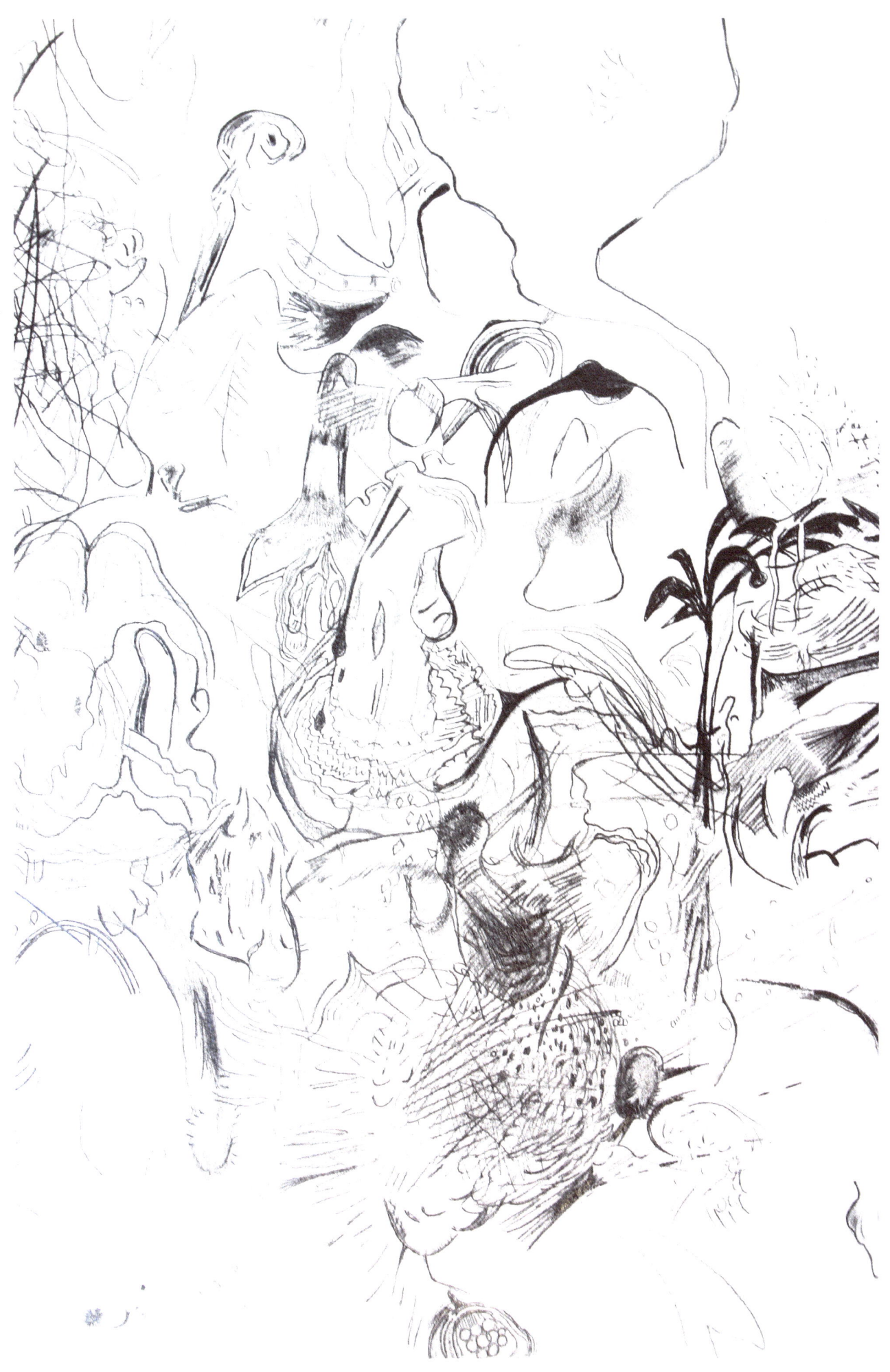

Las Palmas 20/40/60 30"x 22" pencil/paper 2010

< overleaf detail

Untitled May Part I mixed media/paper 30"x 22" 2011

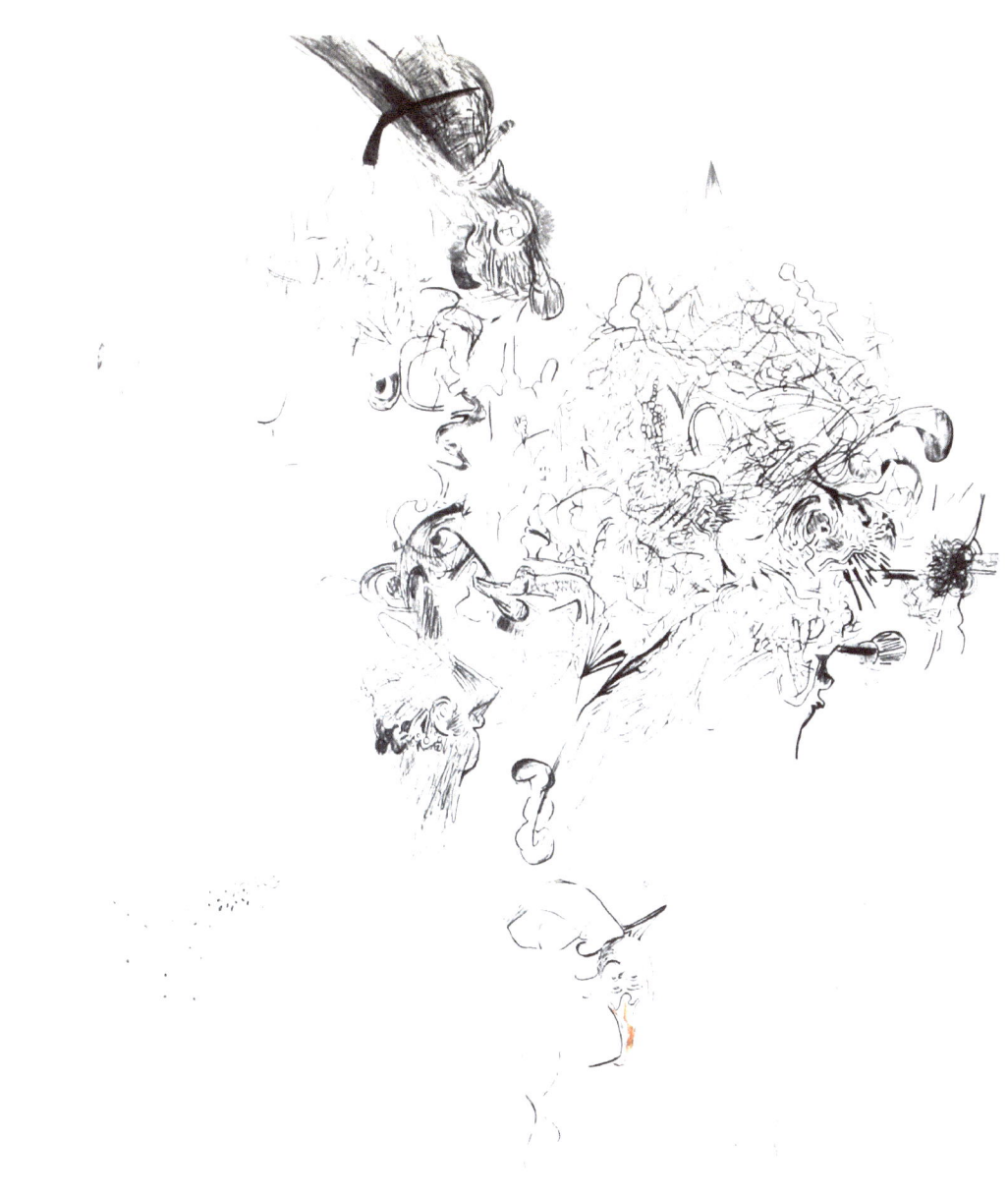

Last Day of September 9/10 pencil/paper 30"x 22" 2010

overleaf detail >

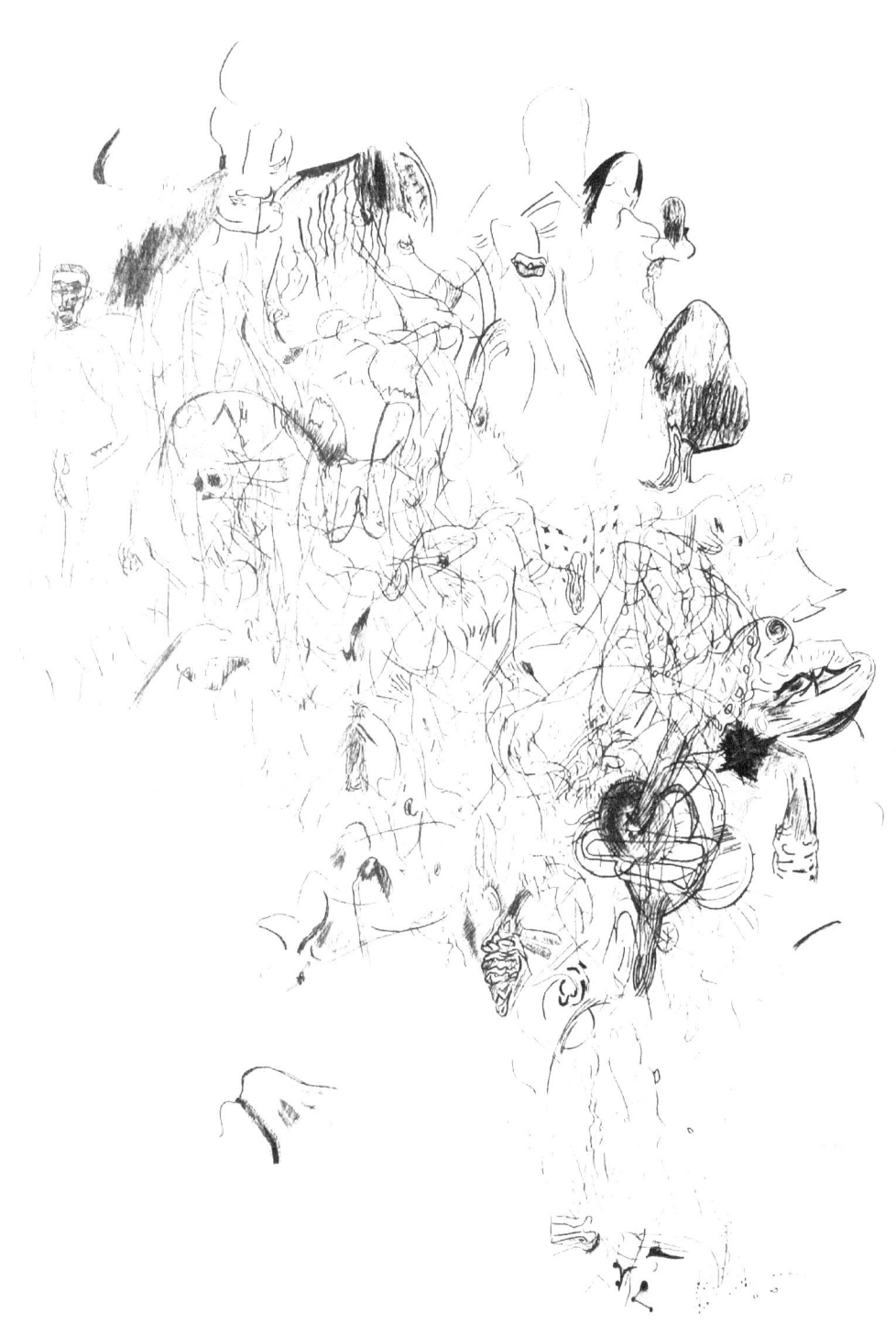

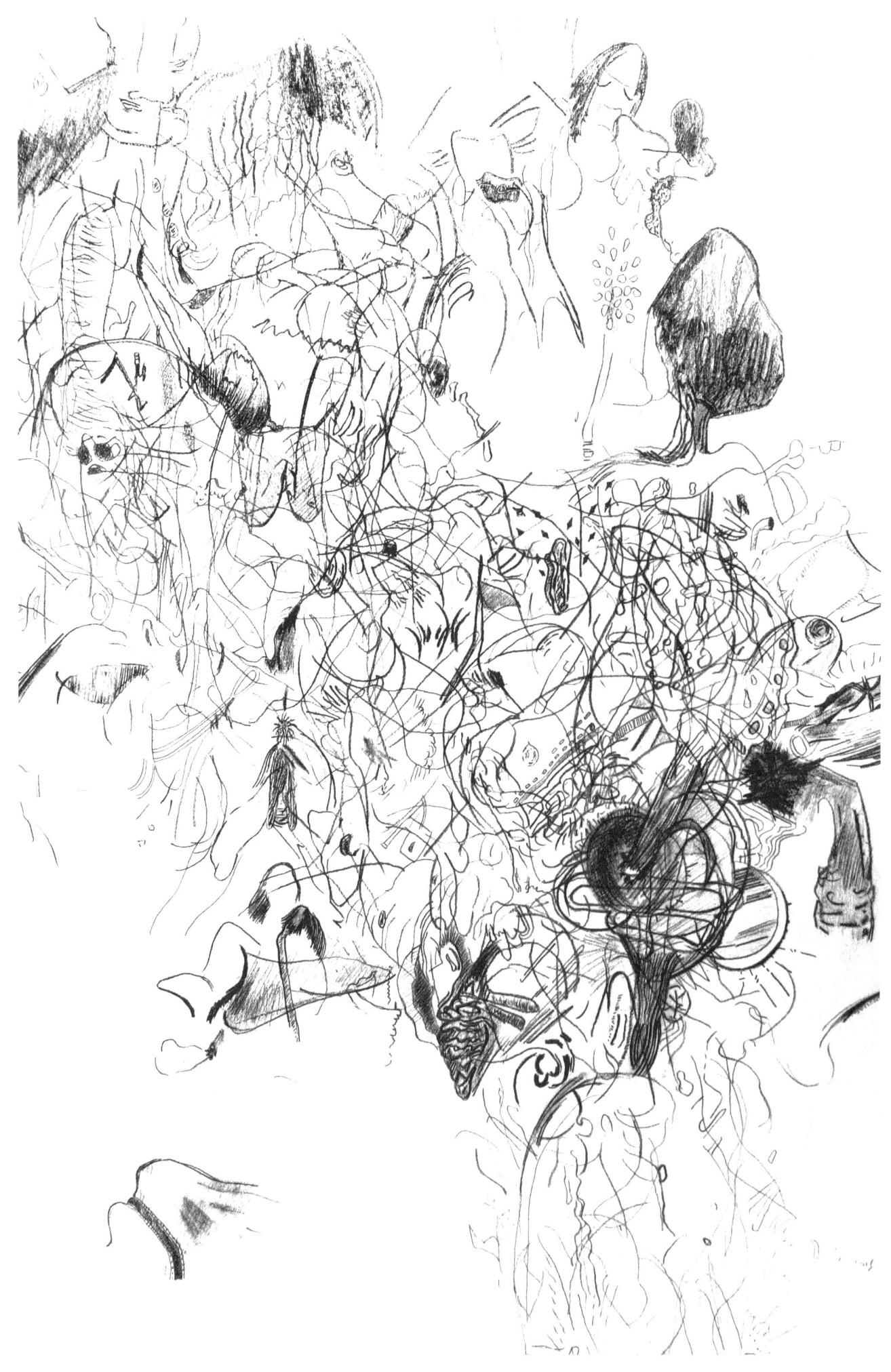

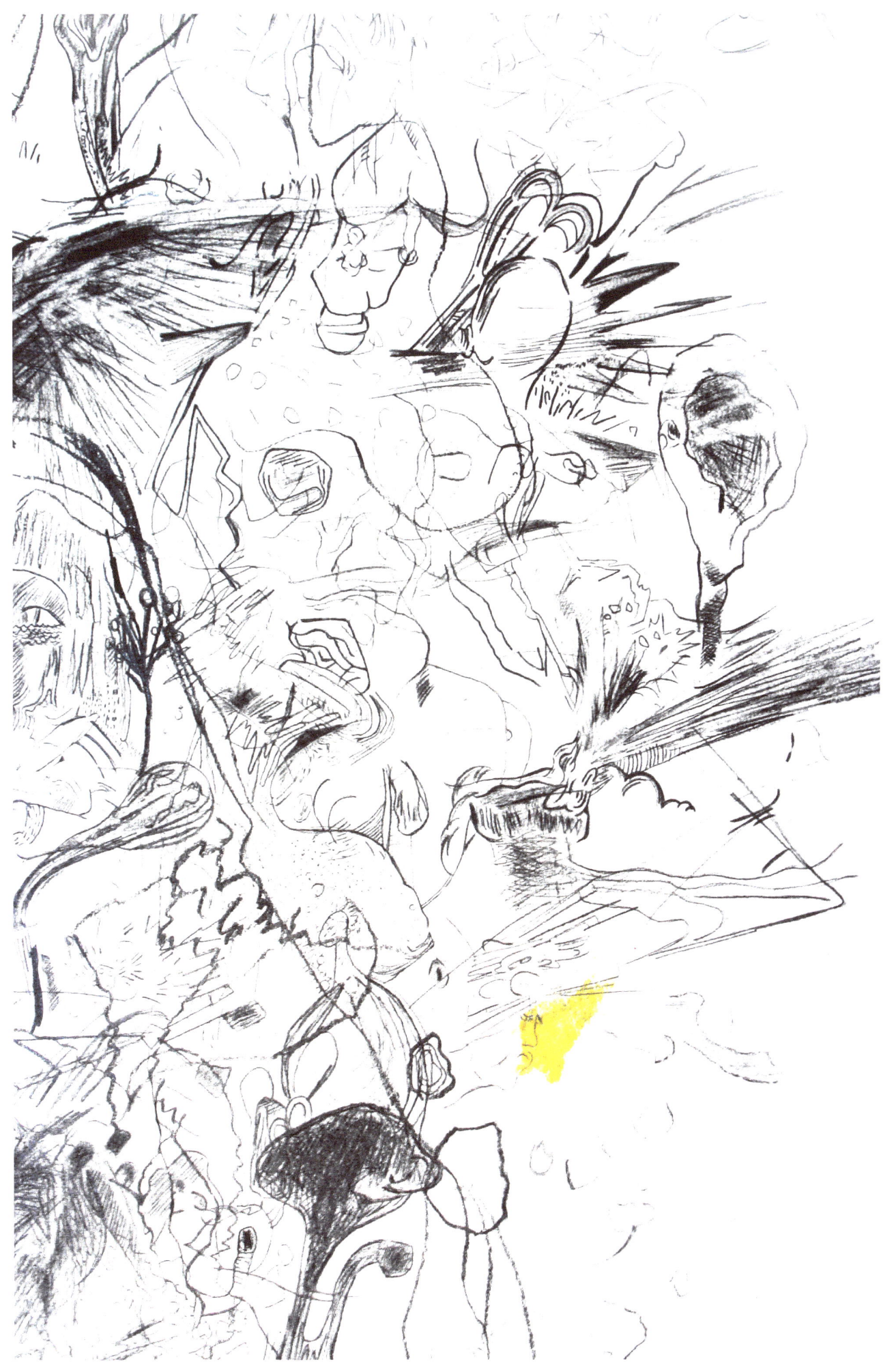

Favorite Part 30"x 22" pencil/paper 2010

< overleaf detail

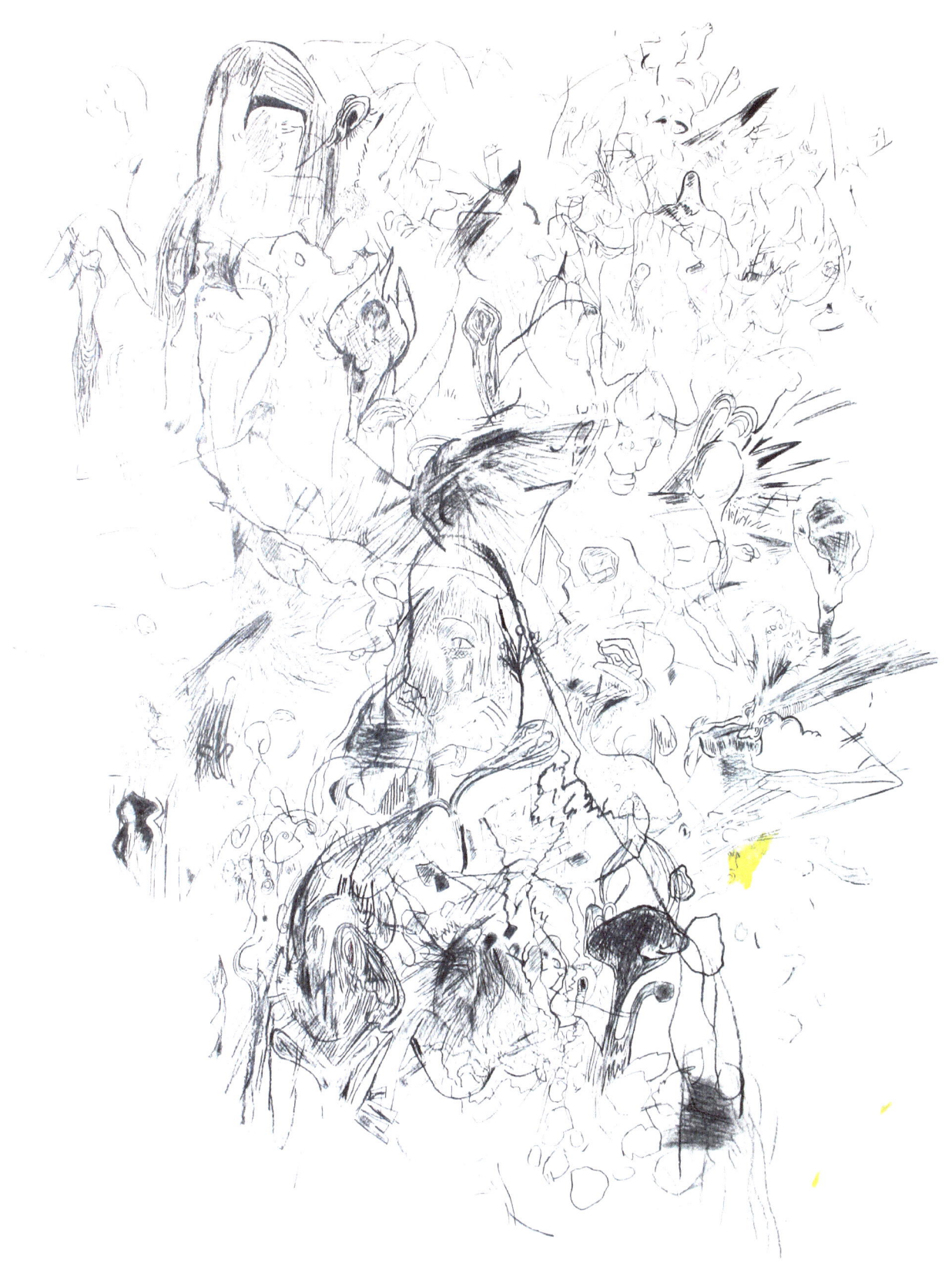

Untitled Part 2 30"x 22" pencil/paper 2011

When Will You Come Back? 30"x 22" pencil/paper 2010

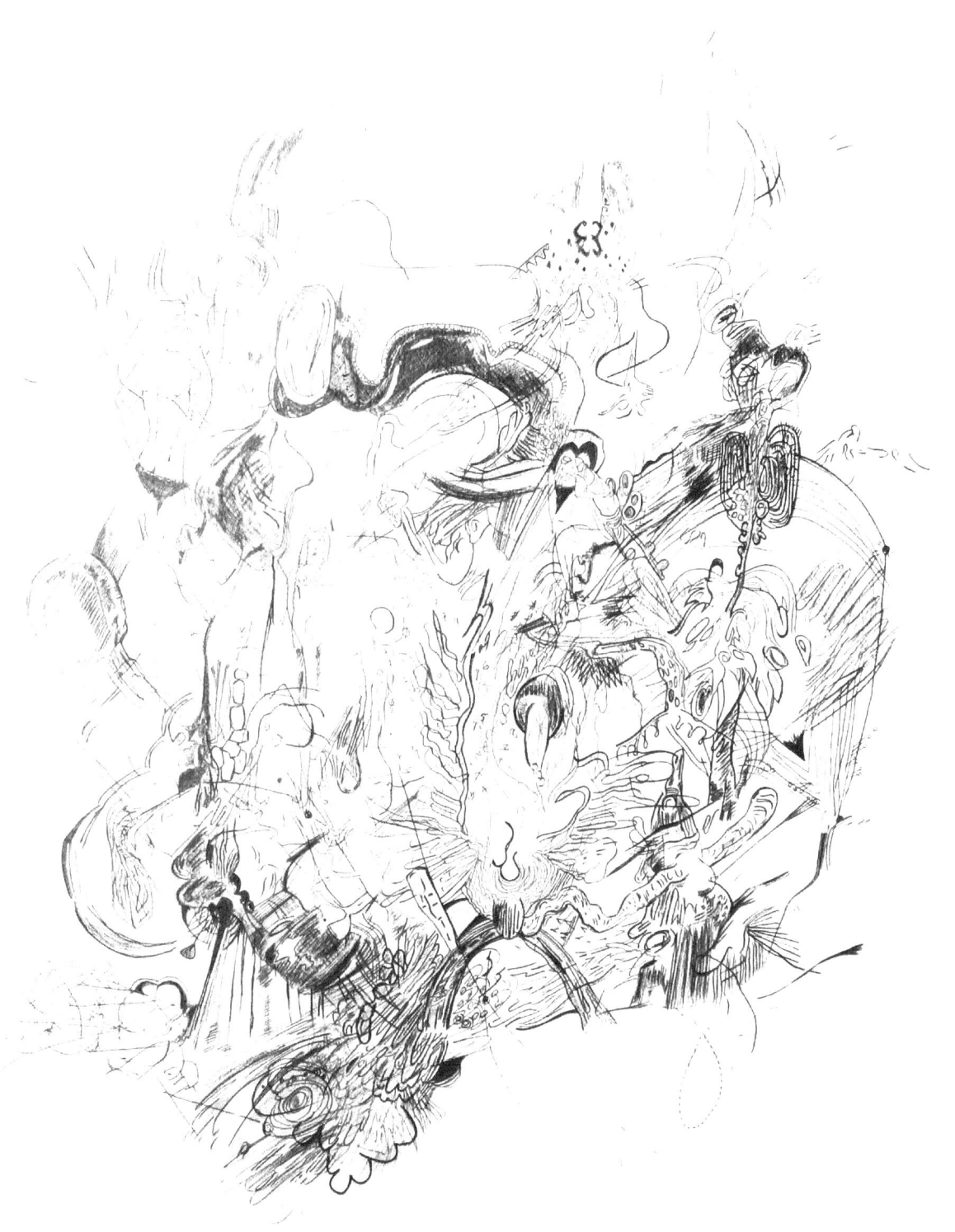

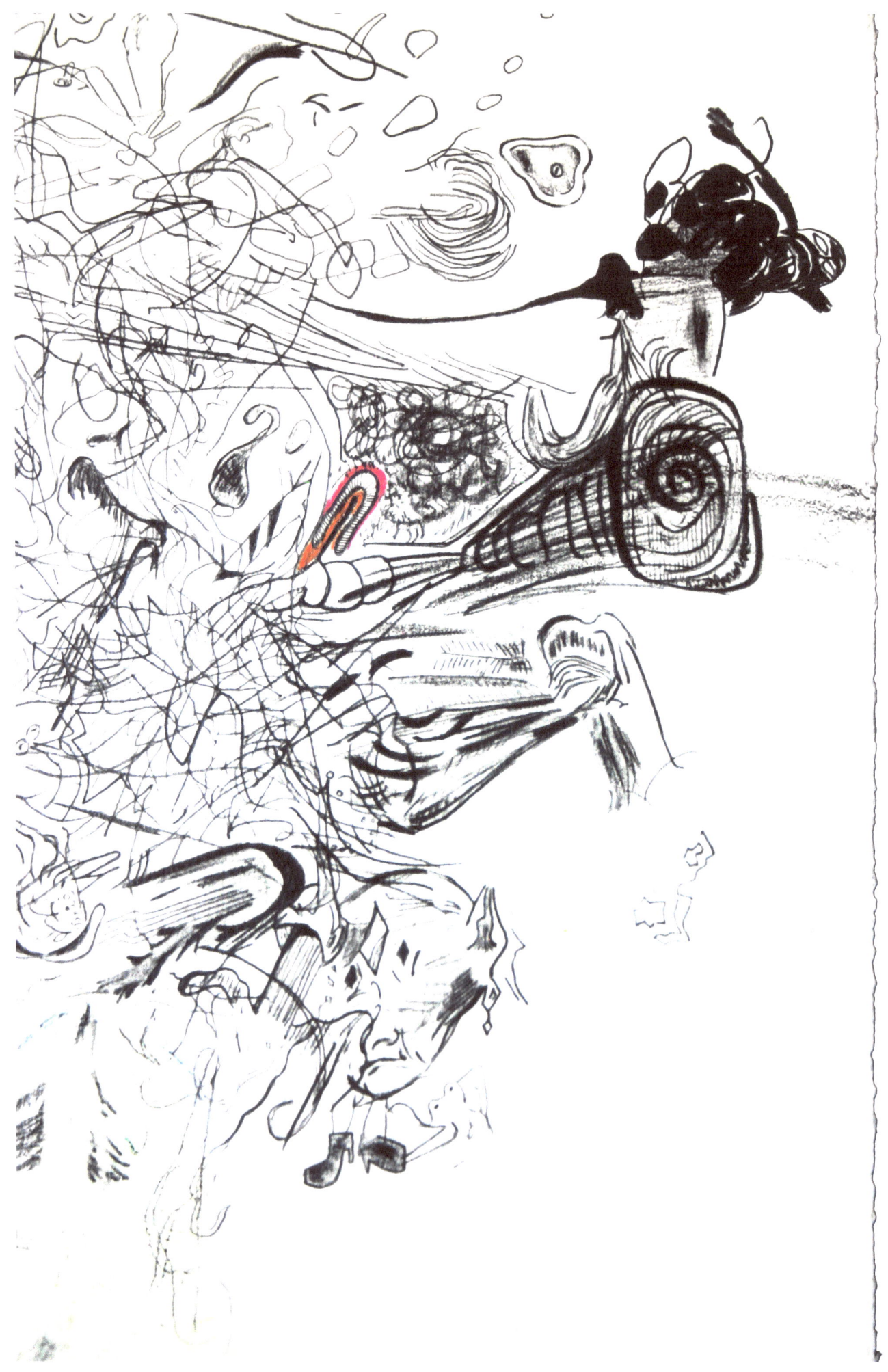

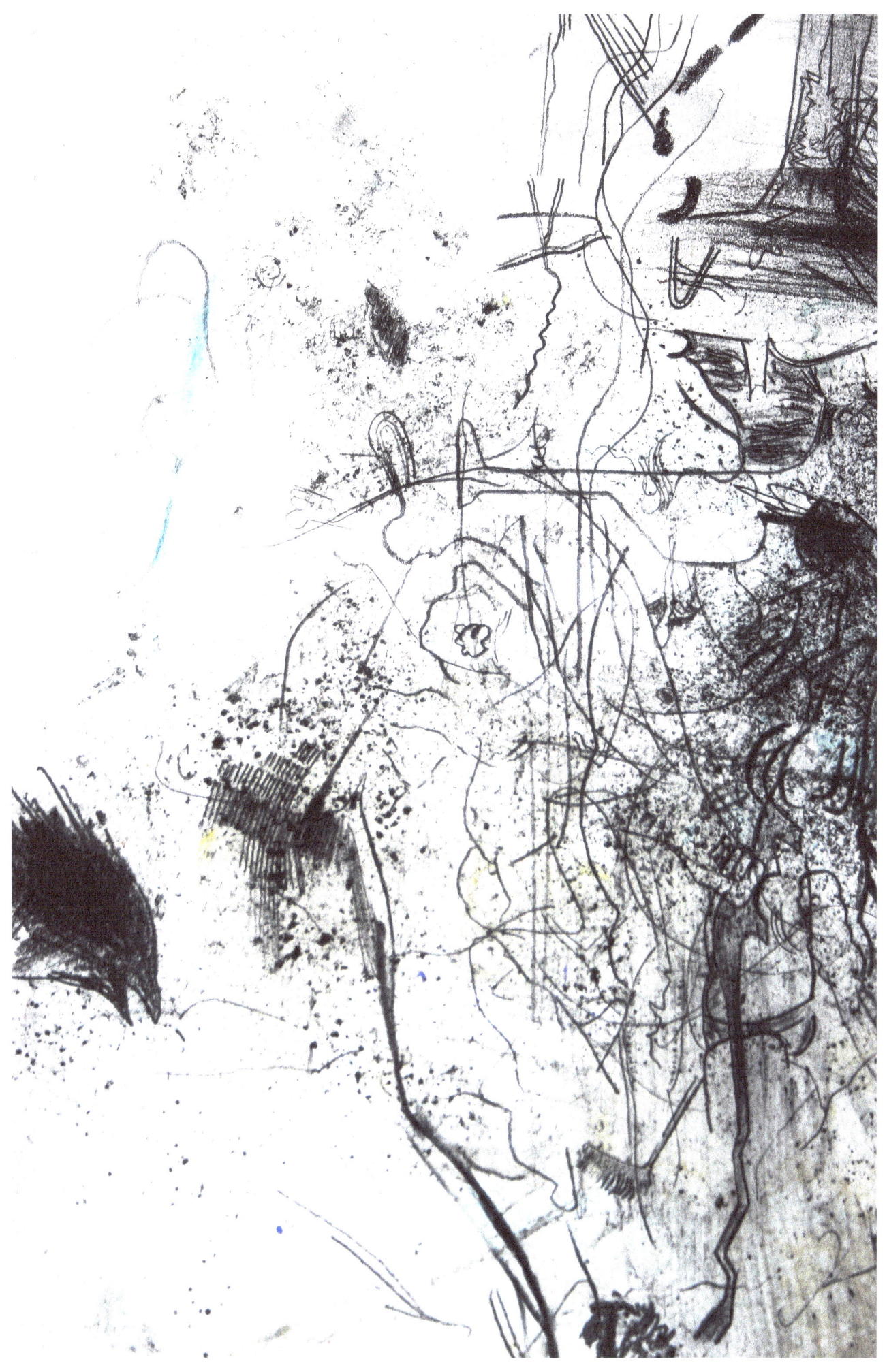

to C.L. NY 2011 mixed media/paper 30"x 22" 2011

< overleaf details

A Love Supreme mixed media/paper 30"x 22" 2011

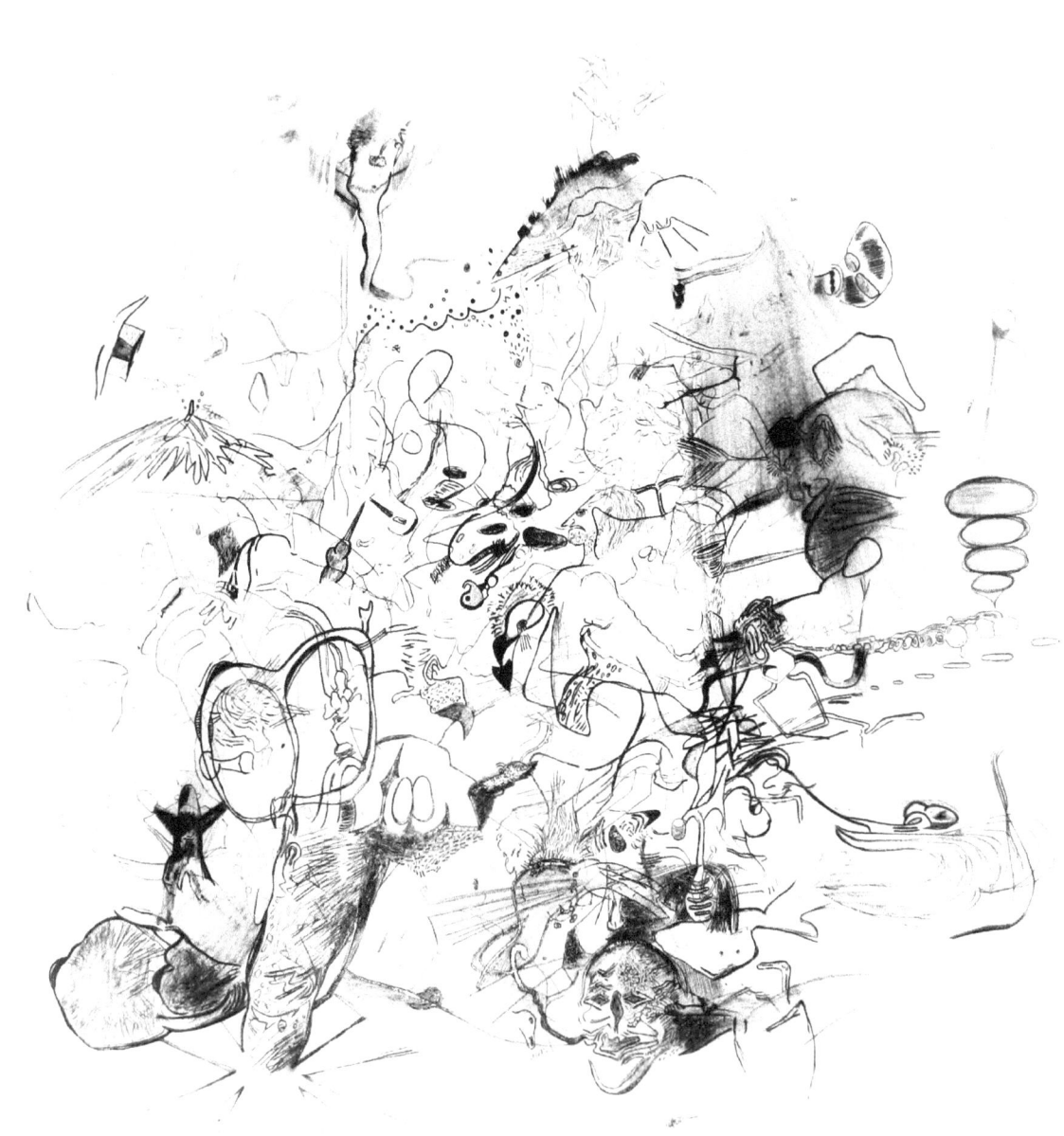

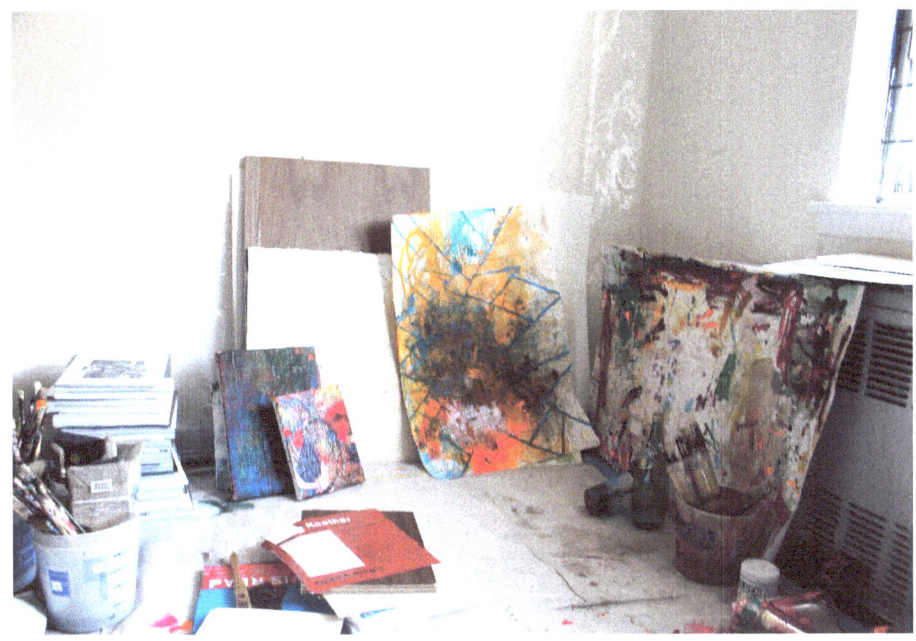

This book is a record of twenty-seven works on paper executed at the end of Hector G. Romero's time in New York City from July 2009–July 2011, when he lived in his studio apartment in Queens.

The apartment consisted of two long, blank walls facing each other, with two windows on the short wall that joined them. Kitchen, bathroom, closet were all pushed behind and out of the way into the little hall-space you entered from. He would only use them as much as he had to—the space was for drawing in. He didn't use the walls for drawing; an air-mattress could be stood against one of them so he could have more floor space, but the books, cds, dvds, paintings and art supplies were most often stacked and piled on the floor a bit away from them, leaving room. The walls stayed empty and white for the whole time he was there. Hector works on the floor, but one can imagine the clear space of the walls helps him, allows him to focus his thoughts and eventually crowd his ideas down onto the paper.

That is exactly what happened, as he worked consistently day by day, week by week; the drawings accomplished during these two years became his strongest body of work yet.

Hector G. Romero is a person known to many involved in the arts in New York City, but few may know his work. In a dozen-plus years as a fine-art book dealer in Manhattan he has sold, located, and suggested books to thousands of people: critics, writers, art students, studio assistants, curators, tourists, locals and of course many well-known and lesser-known artists. Both within the sphere of his professional position and as an artist, he was able to put this situation to his best advantage, surrounding himself with an ever-growing library of the greatest art of the past and present, and making the most of opportunities to meet and interact with a wide array of arts professionals including some of the artists he most admired. He could, always within the restrictions of his post and with characteristic reserve and tact, discuss their work and the art developments of the moment.

He learned a lot through this experience, but in his own art-making Romero has always followed a resolute and steady path, slowly developing and transforming concepts and form from drawing to drawing. Considering his production throughout these years, you are struck by the profusion and amalgam of varied stimuli as well as by the constancy of his particular vision. His own drawing, though certainly informed and cultivated by his deep and varied knowledge of classical and contemporary art and culture, seems to flow from his head and hand naturally and without artifice or pretense in a constant stream of thought and movement. It is this aspect of honesty and vitality that allows his creative, personal imagery to be as relevant as it is and to communicate so well to us.

Now he has a book of his own and we look forward to many more.

James Pustorino, Editor

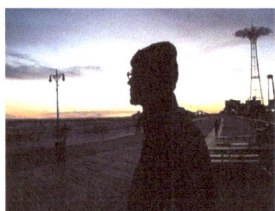

If we consider drawing as a visual language, then Hector Romero's are certainly essays, each one frothing over with impressions, unique characters, personal experiences; densely layered, packed together into captivating narratives and executed with a directness and elegance worthy of an ancient Zen calligrapher. These complex combinations of marks and movements, various pencils and paints, recall elements of graffiti art, surrealism, action painting and comic strip art but create their own, ever-evolving aesthetic form.

Hector G. Romero works with many mediums on both canvas and paper. Before his sojourn in Woodside, Queens, he had been painting and drawing in Brooklyn, NY, for 13 years. Previously, he worked in Los Angeles where he received his MFA at UCLA. He was an integral part of the band "The Charles Ray Experience" known for their eclectic sound collage work. His current work can be described as Urban Surrealism, heavily influenced by his New York City environment. Romero now lives in El Paso, Texas.

photo: Laurie Hefner

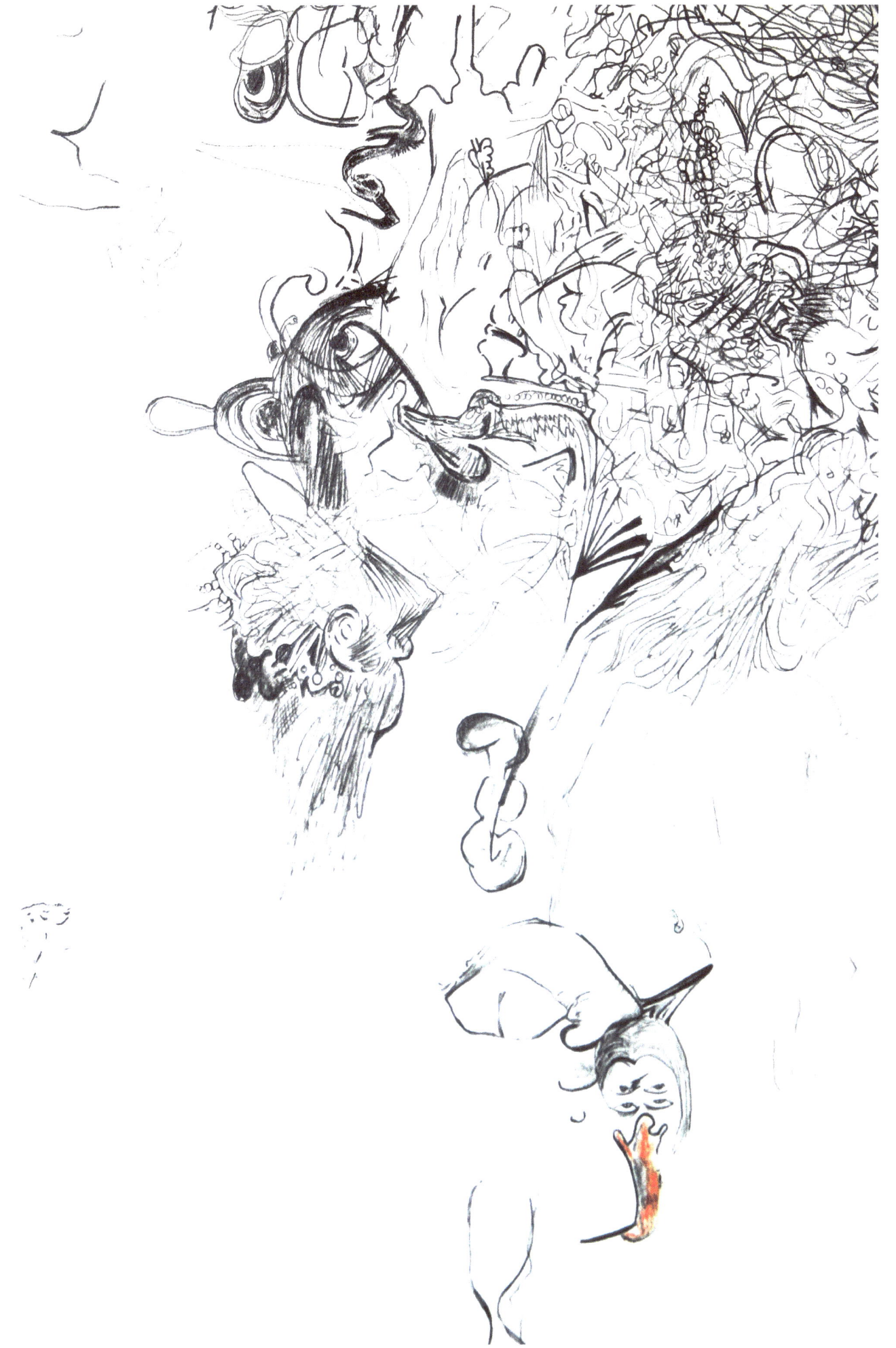

NEW DRAWING

presents series of innovative, current images
from artists whose work explores and expands
the visual and conceptual language of drawing.

Other books in the Series include:
Jill Scipione: Skullnotebook
Carl Vierow: Detective at Red Castle Pier and Other Drawings
James Pustorino: Universechild

Victory Hall Press

is a division of Victory Hall Inc., a not-for-
profit arts organization producing exhibitions,
events, education programs, public projects
and publications, based in the NJ/NY metro
area.
Visit our website at www.victoryhallpress.org

New Drawing

September 2011

Victory Hall Press

Editor: James Pustorino

ISBN-13: 978-0615515311
ISBN-10: 0615515312

Copyright © 2011 by Victory Hall Press

website: www.victoryhallpress.org

contact: victoryhall1@msn.com

Victory Hall Inc. 74 W46 St
Bayonne, NJ 07002
www.victoryhall.org

< *frontispiece and verso of essay:* I Thought She Was Thinking Of Me mixed/media/paper 2010

< *verso of bio page:* Untitled May Part I mixed media/paper 30"x 22" 2011-detail